Feed Me

Bubbe

RECIPES AND WISDOM FROM AMERICA'S FAVORITE ONLINE GRANDMOTHER

Avrom Honig and Bubbe

RUNNING PRESS
PHILADELPHIA • LONDON

Books published by Running Press are available at special discounts for bulk purchases in the United States by corporations, institutions, and other
organizations. For more information, please contact the Special Markets Department at the Perseus Books Group, 2300 Chestnut Street, Suite 200,
Philadelphia, PA 19103, or call (800) 810-4145, ext. 5000, or e-mail special.markets@perseusbooks.com.

ISBN: 978-0-7624-4188-4
E-book ISBN: 978-0-7624-4371-0
Library of Congress Control Number: 2011931293

9 8 7 6 5 4 3 2 1
Digit on the right indicates the number of this printing

Cover photography by Essdras M. Suarez
Interior photographs provided by the authors
Typography: Minion, Univers, Apple Chancery, Corinthia, and Wingdings

Running Press Book Publishers
A Member of the Perseus Books Group
2300 Chestnut Street
Philadelphia, PA 19103-4371

Visit us on the web!
www.runningpresscooks.com
www.feedmebubbe.com

This book is dedicated to Bubbe's parents, Abe and Molle, who taught the family values of life and living, and to Zadie for being so wonderful on and off the set in his patience and encouragement in every way during the writing of this book.

Contents

Preface

When we first started out making the online video series *Feed Me Bubbe* never in our wildest dreams did we think that we would reach where we are today. Our fans kept asking us for a cookbook, and we really didn't even know where to begin. To help you better understand our journey, we need to start with the first major phone call that we received unexpectedly from Chris Brogan on behalf of him and Jeff Pulver inviting us to go to San Jose, California, for our first-ever appearance at the Video On the Net Fall 2007 Conference. It took a lot of convincing to attend since Bubbe really didn't think anyone would ever want to fly us out with all expenses paid. Avrom really had his hands full explaining that they really and truly wanted to have us be there at the conference. When we arrived they made Bubbe feel like a queen and Avrom like a VIP. Bubbe was recognized wherever she went, with many shocked that Bubbe was the main attraction over all of the technological announcements taking place at the same conference. From there we ended up learning many skills from Steve Garfield and his mother, Millie, who is always a pleasure to see. We owe a big debt of gratitude to Steve, Chris, and Jeff for taking an interest in us, and giving us our chance.

We also want to take the opportunity of recognizing Instant Media for broadcasting our very first show on Friday, June 16, 2006, to a worldwide audience. From there we grew into other networks. There are too many to name but the list includes Blip.tv, Blinkx, Dish and Dine, and even YouTube. On YouTube we ended up receiving more fans that really showed us how dedicated a fan base we have, for which we are grateful. In addition the emails have been a constant reminder and a motivator of why we have continued for so long.

Another special thank you to the various celebrities that have recognized our contributions. This includes Carson Daly, who included us on his Internet program, *It's Your Show*. Carson was even going to play our video on New Year's Eve on NBC. Due to time restraints it never made it to air, but it meant a lot to us anyway that they even were planning on doing that in the first place. In addition, we'd like to thank Food Network star Dave Lieberman, who invited us to do a guest appearance on his online food series entitled *In Search of Real Food*.

The press have always been a pleasure to have over in the kitchen and speak to over the Internet using the Skype program. We must thank our very first interview from George of the *One Minute How To* online show, who is always a pleasure to make an appearance on. To all of the media, including Retirement Living

Television, *Frontline, ABC World News*, etc., thank you for teaching Avrom how to use his media equipment, sharing tricks to improve the production. Little things like unplugging the refrigerator, taking off the phone before shooting, and even how to properly set up lighting have made a real difference. To those in the newspaper industry, your questions and conversations have always been delightful and your general interest in seeing us succeed is heartwarming.

Never in our wildest dreams would we ever think that we would get a column in a magazine and we have to thank *Shalom Magazine* for that opportunity. Even the idea that we can be found on television via JLTV in certain areas is incredible to think about. Even our merchandising from our start with Guertin's Graphics and Awards to now Printfection has been a learning experience. We must take an opportunity of course to thank Zadie, Avrom's grandfather and Bubbe's husband, for all of his work helping with the merchandise and being our #1 PA (production assistant) on the set.

Of course we don't want to leave out those that have helped improve the Web site, from Noam Hassenfeld, who composed our theme song, to Tad Davis, who did a brilliant job redesigning our website. At this point we just wish we could name everyone, including Avrom's friends that took the time to help us out when we just needed that extra bit of support. Most importantly this book is all in thanks to an article that was in the *Boston Globe* that was spotted by our future cookbook writer, Lucy Baker. From there, we were fortunate to work with literary agent Sharon Bowers and Running Press Editor Geoffrey Stone. And how could we forget our amazing photographer Essdras M. Suarez who was extremely patient with us during our very special book photo shoot. Everyone worked really hard, and we poured every memory, taste, and feeling that we could in this book.

We know we are missing people and with any list that can happen but just know we appreciate every contribution, including the requests to fix an issue on the website. This has been a team effort and you are all part of our team, especially those that have helped us along the way as we asked for it through the social networking site Facebook on our fan page. We hope that you enjoy this book with your loved ones and are ready for heartwarming stories, delicious recipes, and even a bissel (little) Yiddish.

Love,

Bubbe and Avrom

Introduction

Are you hungry? Do you need a little nosh? It doesn't matter what you say—I won't take "no" for an answer. I'm a bubbe (that's Yiddish for grandmother) and feeding people is what I do best. In just a minute, I'm going to teach you how to make all of my favorite Jewish recipes, from chicken soup to chocolate-swirled mandel bread. These are the dishes that have nourished and comforted my family for generations. In fact, many of them came over on the ships from Europe and Russia. Now that's what I call time-tested! Big bowls of steaming cabbage and meat borscht; crisp radish salads; and sweet, crunchy *kichlach* (that's Yiddish for puffed sugar cookies) have been sustaining people for hundreds of years—and for good reason. Not only do they taste delicious, they also taste like home.

Don't worry if you're not a gourmet cook. I'm not, either. My recipes are simple and straightforward. I've done my best to explain just how I make each dish from start to finish. So don't worry if you aren't sure how to properly rinse a chicken, soak matzo for matzo brei, or mix ingredients for meatballs—I'll talk you through each and every step. It will be just like your own grandmother is there with you in the kitchen! I promise that if you follow my directions, even you—yes you—can prepare soothing chicken soup, moist and tender beef brisket, and creamy noodle kugel.

All bubbes have a deeply ingrained need to make sure everyone they know is well fed. But I can't stop there—I feel the need to feed people I don't know, too! That's why, at eighty years old, I came out of retirement to star in my own Internet cooking show. I wanted to share everything I know about sweet and sour meatballs, scrambled eggs with lox, and challah bread stuffing with the world. Believe me, after raising children and grandchildren, I know a lot! But before we head for the kitchen, let me tell you a little bit about myself. My hope is that I will remind you of your own grandmother— or the grandmother you always wished for.

My own mother immigrated to America from Russia after World War I. She met my father here, in the United States. I was born in 1926 in a town in New England, where I have lived all my life. Many of my first memories are about food: watching my mother crush Concord grapes to make kosher wine for Passover (she let it ferment in a large ceramic pot that she wedged between the stove and the wall), going with her to the butcher

Bubbe's mother, Molle, in 1925

Bubbe's father in Russia during World War I

to buy calves feet for *pitcha,* or to the fruit market for juicy tomatoes and cucumbers that she would slice and layer in the most delicious sandwiches.

I bumped into my husband Zadie (that's Yiddish for grandfather) walking from the synagogue on Yom Kippur when I was twenty years old. After we were married, I suddenly found myself in charge of preparing a hot meal each night. At first it was difficult. And wouldn't you know, I burned a few pot roasts and once had to throw an entire lemon sponge cake in the trash. Raising a family and working certainly kept me busy full

time. Like any mother today, I had to find the perfect balance. It was not easy to learn to adapt my recipes to fit a busy lifestyle, but with lots of patience and practice, I became a terrific cook.

Now I'm famous for dishes like my potato latkes, brisket, and blintzes. These days there is nothing I love more than to feed my entire extended family on various occasions, including Shabbos meals, dinners on the holidays, or really anytime at all, be it birthdays, anniversaries, or celebrating family accomplishments. Nobody ever goes hungry when they come to my house. I always

The members of our family circle

have a plate of tuna or egg salad sandwiches and some hot chocolate always ready. Already had lunch? Then surely you still have room for a cookie, or two, or three. Nobody ever leaves empty-handed either. Just try and walk out the door without a tin filled with marble mandel bread or a large slice of pineapple sponge cake for the road.

Like I said, I've lived in the same New England town for my entire life. I never had giant aspirations or dreams of fame. But my grandson, Avrom, was different. In 2006 Avrom graduated college and was looking for a job in the media industry. He tried his best to make a demo reel that he could bring with him to interviews, but he wasn't satisfied with whatever he made. One evening during dinner Avrom and his Dad were discussing the demo and Avrom explained he wasn't happy with it. His Dad suggested, "Since Bubbe is always sending over some kind of food why not just make a video of her cooking?" During the discussion, Avrom told me about how he wanted the perfect title, and he and his father spent time working out the name. Every title proposed was rejected to the point that his father got upset and said to Avrom, "Why don't you just call the stupid thing *Feed Me Bubbe*!" Avrom was delighted, and the next morning he came to visit and brought his camera along and patiently explained to me how I could help. I would do anything to help my grandchildren, especially if it meant it would help them find a job. On the first show we recorded, I made Jelly Jammies, which is my easy version of classic Jewish strudel. They are so delicious, filled with raisins, nuts, and jam with just a pinch of lemon zest, perfect with a cup of tea. I guess others thought so, too, because more than twenty thousand people watched the episode on YouTube. I could not believe it. We started to get emails from all over the globe!

Of course at that time I knew absolutely nothing about computers. *What does a Bubbe need with computers and technology?* In the same way that I've tried to educate Avrom about cooking, I found myself receiving an education on the basics of computers. I always thought I got along fine for nearly eighty years without a cell phone or the World Wide Web. But then I started thinking about all the new kitchen inventions I use every day that weren't around when I was young, like microwaves, electric mixers, and slow cookers. Maybe I should learn a thing or two about the Internet after all . . . and I'm very glad I did. We received so many emails from people requesting more videos and asking if I could demonstrate how to make various recipes in future episodes. Who would ever think that at this age I would be so busy making videos and trying very hard to keep up answering so many emails no matter how long it takes? This was never supposed to be an actual show, but with so many requests I've taken

Bubbe holding one of her daughters at a family gathering

Bubbe giving a cooking lesson

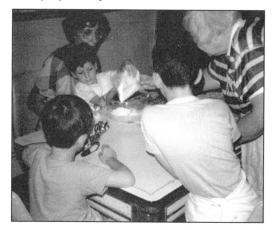
More cooking lessons

this experience as a great opportunity to spend time with Avrom and saw nothing wrong with making more episodes. It's amazing to me that there are so many people out there who need my help. They don't know how to stuff cabbage! They've never tasted chopped liver! They can't remember the ingredients for matzo brei!

Avrom Honig and Bubbe

In my wildest dreams, I never thought *Feed Me Bubbe* would be such a success. Avrom and I have been written about in newspapers and interviewed on the evening news. Reporters have asked me why they think my show is so popular, and in all honesty I'm not really sure. However, when I reflect back on all of the messages, I can see how viewers see in me their own grandmother, who is always there to provide a few warm words of encouragement. Also, lots of people have fond memories of being in their grandmother's kitchen watching her prepare roast chicken, tzimis, and gefilte fish, but don't know how to prepare them on their own. Now I'm here to show you how.

Of course, my recipes are kosher (more about that in a minute) but even if you're not Jewish, and don't know your *schmaltz* from your *gribenes*, I promise you will find many dishes to love and prepare again and again. Pretty soon, you will be flipping salmon patties and making chopped liver to rival any deli's.

Following a tradition of our video show, at the end of each recipe I'm going to teach you a Yiddish word of the day. Yiddish is a Jewish dialect that was once a major Eastern European language spoken by millions of people. It has roots in Hebrew and German. You might think you don't know any Yiddish, but chances are you hear it every day. Common words like *shlep*, *chutzpah*, and *schmooze* are actually Yiddish. And I'm going to teach you 100 more words and phrases. Ready? Here is the first one:

Es Gezunterhait! It means eat in good health.

Time to start cooking; let's begin . . .

Quick Notes on Keeping Kosher

Just as you don't have to be Italian to love spaghetti and meatballs or Chinese to love steamed dumplings, you don't have to be Jewish to enjoy kosher food. As you flip through the recipes in this book, you will notice that each one is marked with a (D), (M), or (P). Those letters tell you whether the dish is dairy (or *milchik* in Yiddish), meat (*fleishik*), or neutral (*pareve*). The first rule of keeping kosher is that dairy and meat cannot be eaten together. Neutral foods can be eaten with either dairy or meat.

A lot of people think that keeping kosher is difficult and time-consuming. But actually it's quite simple. I've been keeping kosher my whole life. Jews keep kosher for many reasons. Of course because the Torah says so! Another reason is that following the laws gives the act of preparing and eating food special religious meaning. Each time I sit down to a delicious meal, I am reminded of my faith, and what it means to me to be Jewish. I think that is something that is very important. Even if you aren't Jewish, I would encourage you to reflect a little bit over your dinner each night. I promise if you do, your food will taste even more wonderful.

Here is a brief outline of the Jewish dietary laws. You certainly don't have to follow them to enjoy all my recipes, but they are good to know.

Kashrut

The body of Jewish laws that deal with food and food preparation is called *Kashrut*. *Kashrut* comes from the Hebrew word for "proper" or "correct." Foods that are in accordance with these laws are kosher. Foods that aren't are *treif*, which comes from the Hebrew word for "torn." During Passover, there are additional laws. Some foods that are kosher most of the year are not kosher for Passover, like my delicious Apple Cinnamon Bread Kugel, made with challah.

Animals

Kosher meats include beef, lamb, goat, deer, and bison. Non-kosher meats include pork and rabbit. Most poultry is kosher, like turkey, duck, goose, and of course chicken (where would we be without chicken soup with matzo balls?). Any fish with fins and scales is kosher, including salmon, tuna, cod, and herring. Catfish, swordfish, and shellfish like shrimp, oysters, and lobster are examples of fish that are not kosher. Consult a rabbi for more information.

Kosher animals must also be slaughtered according to Jewish law. This process is called *shechitah*, and involves a quick, deep cut across the throat of the animal with a special knife. This method is widely recognized as the most humane way to slaughter an animal, and many people who don't keep kosher buy kosher meat for this reason.

The Torah also prohibits eating blood. Most of the blood is drained from the animal at the time of the slaughter. The rest must be removed by broiling, salting, or soaking the meat.

Fruit and Vegetables

All fruit and vegetables are kosher, with the exception of grape products like grape juice and wine. For grape juice and wine to be kosher, they must be made under special conditions. Kosher grape juice is readily available in every supermarket, and there are many delicious kosher wines out there. Ask your local wine merchant for a recommendation.

Separating Meat and Dairy

The Torah prohibits eating meat or poultry and dairy together. There are many interpretations as to eating fish and milk together. After eating meat, you must wait at least three hours before eating dairy; however, many wait for six hours, but use your own discretion. Also, after eating dairy, all you need to do is drink a little water to rinse out your mouth and have a few bites of a neutral food, like bread, before eating meat; however, follow the rules according to your discretion and your beliefs.

Kosher laws also state that you must have separate utensils, plates, pots, and pans for cooking meat and dairy. So, for example, you can't make beef stew in the same pot you use to heat milk. I have two separate sets of everything in my house: one for meat and one for dairy, along with extra cooking equipment for when I want to make pareve recipes. It sounds like a lot, but once you have everything set up in your cabinets it's easy.

The Importance of Pareve

In true kosher cooking, meat and dairy should never be combined. Pareve margarine is made up of 100 percent vegetable oil. Dairy margarine has milk as one of the ingredients plus perhaps added vegetable oil. This is why when cooking a meat or dairy meal, if the recipe requires butter or margarine, I substitute it with pareve margarine. To avoid even the appearance of such a combination I will never put pareve margarine on the same table as a meat meal. However, there are people in many kosher homes that will put out pareve margarine with meat, but they will make sure to serve it with the label visible so that everyone can see that the margarine is in fact pareve. When you read the recipes you may find in certain ones that I mention to use pareve margarine. Some products like chocolate or coffee creamer are normally assumed to be a dairy product. However, there are several brands that are pareve and contain no dairy. When shopping for margarine, it is very easy to find the symbols that indicate whether or not it is pareve. There will be a "D" or "Dairy" or "Pareve" printed on the top or side.

Kosher Certification

Contrary to what many people think, the process of certifying something kosher doesn't involve a rabbi blessing the food. Instead, the ingredients, preparation, and place (like the bakery, or factory) must be examined to make sure they all meet kosher standards. Foods that meet these standards are marked with a hekhsher. These days, the majority of packaged supermarket foods have some type of kosher certification. The symbols of kosher certifications can be tough to find, but with practice it becomes easier. Even today I struggle with new products since it's up to the manufacturer as to where they put it. Usually it can be found on the front of the package where you have the logos, text, and pictures of the product. If it's not there look where the nutrition information is; sometimes it can be found there. If you still can't find it, make sure to check every part of the box to be certain. You may find the words "dairy," "meat," "pareve,"

or even "kosher for Passover" appearing as well next to the symbol. Consult a synagogue or Jewish organization in your area to supply you with the kosher symbols for your community.

For reference in this book we will be using the following symbols next to the title of each recipe.

P = Pareve (neutral food containing no meat or dairy)

M = contains meat

D = contains dairy

⊛ = Passover dish

Breakfast

Even though breakfast foods aren't hard to make, lots of people still find them intimidating. They end up eating only cereal or toast each morning. That is such a shame! No bubbe worth her salt would let you get away with skipping breakfast. It's the most important meal of the day! A healthy breakfast provides lots of energy and keeps you feeling full for hours. Plus, there is no better way to wake up than to the aroma of an omelet with lox, onions, and peppers and sweet blueberry buckle (coffee cake) with hot coffee or cocoa. During Passover, when I make my famous Stuffed Matzo Meal Latkes (Pancakes) or Savory Matzo Brei (Fried Matzo), everyone in my family jumps out of bed excited for a taste.

There are so many other delicious and healthy options. Just make sure to have a cup of coffee before you start cooking. Relax and take your time, and I promise whatever you make will come out tasting wonderful.

One of the dishes we got the most requests for on *Feed Me Bubbe* was blintzes. All our fans wanted to know how to make traditional Jewish blintzes just like the ones they remembered from childhood, or like the best ones they had ever tasted at a restaurant. Well, I have to admit that when my children were young I made them often, but then later on when the children were out of the house, I got a little lazy when it came to making blintzes for Zadie and me. You can buy frozen ones at the supermarket, and they taste pretty good! But when I knew we were going to devote an entire Internet show to blintzes, I needed to brush up on my skills. I searched through all my boxes and folders of recipes and found a tiny scrap of paper with my family's blintz recipe on it. What a wonderful surprise! I didn't even know I had it, and that little piece of paper brought back so many memories.

In fact, I was so excited to work on the video that I wanted to include our family's favorites, including apple, blueberry, and the traditional cheese fillings. Even though normally served during the holiday of Shavuot, secretly I like to serve blintzes for a special occasion as a breakfast treat or for a brunch. The apple and blueberry can even be served as a dessert if you add whipped cream or ice cream on the side.

Of course, no chapter on Jewish breakfast would be complete without a recipe involving lox. I just love every kind of lox, from the milder-tasting Nova smoked salmon you can buy today to the true salty lox I remember gobbling up as a little girl. I have three favorite ways to eat it: one is with eggs, onions, and peppers; the second is on a bagel (and you don't need a recipe for that!); and the third is rolled up in lavash bread with cream cheese, olives, and fresh vegetables. My Lox and Cream Cheese Rollups are so delicious, once you make the recipe I know you will start eating them for breakfast all the time—and lunch, too.

Well, that's enough chitchat. Let's head to the kitchen!

Savory Matzo Brei (Fried Matzo)

This savory matzo brei makes a very satisfying breakfast or lunch. Of course, it's perfect for Passover, but you can enjoy it any time you like. For a change I always serve fried matzo with our family favorite, cherry preserves. My grandchildren said they would like to try other toppings, such as mushrooms, peppers, and onions, but feel free to add in whatever vegetables you have in your refrigerator.

Makes 1 serving

- 2 teaspoons plus 1 tablespoon vegetable oil, divided
- ¼ cup diced onions
- ¼ of a large red or green bell pepper, diced
- 2 or 3 large button mushrooms, sliced
- 1 large egg or two large egg whites
- 2 tablespoons water plus more for soaking
- 2 whole matzos

Heat 2 teaspoons of vegetable oil in a medium frying pan over medium heat. Add the onions and sauté for a minute. Add the bell pepper and cook for another minute. Add the mushrooms and stir and cook until the vegetables are lightly browned. Set aside.

Whisk the egg in a bowl with 2 tablespoons water. Place the matzo in another bowl and add enough water to cover it. Let the matzo soak for a minute or two, then break it into large pieces with your hands and add to the egg mixture. Stir the matzo with a fork and let the mixture soak for 1 to 2 minutes longer.

Heat the remaining tablespoon of vegetable oil in a second frying pan and pour in the matzo mixture. Be careful so that it doesn't splatter! Fry the matzo on one side until it is set and a little brown at the edges, about 3 minutes. Carefully flip the matzo (don't worry too much if it breaks) and continue to fry for another minute or two. Place the matzo on a plate.

Top the matzo with the vegetable mixture and serve hot.

yiddish word of the day ✡ **geshmak = tasty or delicious**

Stuffed Matzo Meal Latkes (Pancakes)

These latkes are traditionally served during Passover, but I think they are so delicious they deserve to be eaten all year round. Is there a better way to wake up in the morning than to the comforting sounds and smells of your bubbe making latkes? I like my latkes with cherry jam best, but use whatever flavor is your favorite. If you are preparing them for Passover, make sure the jam or jelly is certified kosher for Passover.

Makes 4 servings

3 large eggs, separated

½ cup matzo meal

½ teaspoon kosher salt

½ cup water

Vegetable oil for frying

7 to 10 teaspoons jam or jelly

Whisk the egg yolks for a few minutes in a large bowl until they are pale yellow. In another large bowl, stir together the matzo meal, salt, and water. Add the matzo meal mixture to the egg yolks and stir until the mixture is well blended.

In a medium-size bowl, beat the egg whites with an electric mixer until they hold stiff peaks. Fold the egg whites into the matzo meal mixture with a rubber spatula or a large wooden spoon. Do this carefully so that you don't accidentally deflate them.

Heat ¼ inch of vegetable oil in a large frying pan. Drop tablespoonfuls of batter into the hot oil and flatten them with the back of a spoon. Carefully place 1 teaspoon of jam or jelly in the center of each latke and then top the latke with a little bit more batter. Fry the latkes for 4 minutes, until they are golden. Flip the latkes over and fry for another 3 minutes. (Work in batches if you need to, and keep adding more vegetable oil to the pan!) Transfer the latkes to a plate covered with paper towels to drain. Serve the latkes hot.

yiddish word of the day ✡ **Gutn morgn! = Good morning!**

Cheese Blintzes

When my children were little, I used to prepare these blintzes (which are sort of like crêpes) all the time. The original recipe is printed on a tiny scrap of paper that has become stained with ingredients over the years. Holding it in my hands brings back so many memories! You can eat blintzes for breakfast, lunch, dinner, or even dessert! Blintzes are especially served on Shavuot, which is a two-day holiday generally around the end of May or June. It celebrates the time Moses received the Torah on Mount Sinai.

Makes 9 to 10 servings
(2 per serving)

Batter

2 large eggs, lightly beaten

1 cup all-purpose flour

2 cups water

4 ounces (1 stick) margarine,
  for greasing, divided

Filling

1 (8-ounce) package cream
  cheese, softened

8 ounces farmer's cheese
  or drained cottage cheese

2 large eggs, lightly beaten

1 teaspoon granulated sugar

¼ teaspoon cinnamon

½ teaspoon kosher salt

For the batter: Always crack your eggs individually into a small bowl to make sure they are okay. Pour them into a larger bowl and beat slightly. Then, add a little flour to the eggs and stir a little. Add a little flour alternately with a little water and continue stirring until a very thin smooth batter is formed. I find that sometimes it's easier to mix the batter with a spoon than a fork. Place a smooth dish towel on the table or counter.

Heat an 8-inch nonstick frying pan over medium heat. Measure 3 tablespoons of batter into a small dish. Take the pan off the heat (do not turn off the stove) and quickly grease the pan with a little margarine. I use a piece of waxed paper or pastry brush to lightly coat the pan evenly. After greasing the pan, quickly pour in the batter. Tilt the pan so that the batter coats the bottom in an even, thin layer, returning the pan to the burner. Don't worry if the first few don't come out right. It's all about developing a partnership with the frying pan. Even the best of us do not succeed with the first ones. Cook until the pancake is dry and set at the edges and releases easily from the pan, 1 to 2 minutes. Flip the

yiddish word of the day ✡ **yontev** = holiday

frying pan over onto the cloth dish towel, making sure to hit the pan against the counter top to help loosen the blintz, and let the blintz cool. Repeat with remaining batter, coating the pan with margarine for each blintz. Be sure to stir the batter every time you measure it out because the flour and liquid tend to separate.

To make the filling, combine the cream cheese and farmer's cheese in a large bowl. Work the cheese together with a fork until it's softened. Add the eggs, sugar, cinnamon, and salt and give it a good stir until well combined and light and fluffy.

To make the blintzes, take 1 rounded tablespoon of filling and place it in the center of each pancake. Fold the top edge to the center, covering the filling. Then fold in one side and then the other side and then fold it up, forming a square. Repeat with remaining filling and pancakes.

Heat a large frying pan. I like to use medium heat for the burner. When hot add 1 to 2 tablespoons of margarine. Let it melt and then add the blintzes. Working in batches, place the blintzes, seam side down, in the pan and fry until golden brown, 2 to 4 minutes per side. You can serve them with sour cream or yogurt and a mixture of cinnamon and sugar or fruit preserves.

Garnish

Sour cream or yogurt and a mixture of cinnamon and sugar or fruit preserves for serving

Apple Blintzes

These apple blintzes are great to serve when you have company coming for brunch. You can prepare the blintzes early in the morning, and then just pop them in the oven for about 20 minutes when your guests arrive. They also make a delicious dessert with vanilla ice cream. I make them most often in the fall, when apples are in season (and on sale!).

*Makes 9 to 10 servings
(2 per serving)*

Batter

2 large eggs, lightly beaten

1 cup all-purpose flour

2 cups water

4 ounces (1 stick) pareve margarine, for greasing, divided

Filling

1 large egg white

1½ cups finely chopped peeled apples

¼ cup granulated sugar

½ teaspoon cinnamon

Garnish

3 tablespoons pareve margarine

3 tablespoons light brown sugar

For the batter: Always crack your eggs individually into a small bowl to make sure they are okay. Pour them into a larger bowl and beat slightly. Then, add a little flour to the eggs and stir a little. Add a little flour alternately with a little water and continue stirring until a very thin smooth batter is formed. I find that sometimes it's easier to mix the batter with a spoon than a fork. Place a smooth dish towel on the table or counter.

Heat an 8-inch nonstick frying pan over medium heat. Measure 3 tablespoons of batter into a small dish. Take the pan off the heat (do not turn off the stove) and quickly grease the pan with a little pareve margarine. I use a piece of waxed paper or pastry brush to lightly coat the pan evenly. After greasing the pan, return it to the burner and quickly pour in the batter. Tilt the pan so that the batter coats the bottom in an even, thin layer, returning the pan to the burner. Don't worry if the first few don't come out right. It's all about developing a partnership with the frying pan. Even the best of us do not succeed with the first ones. Cook until the pancake is dry and set at the edges and releases easily from the pan, 1 to 2 minutes. Flip the frying pan over onto the cloth dish towel, making sure to hit the pan against the counter top to help loosen the blintz, and let the blintz cool. Repeat with remaining batter, coating the pan with pareve margarine for each blintz. Be sure to stir the batter every time you measure it out because the flour and liquid tend to separate.

To make the filling, beat the egg white with an electric mixer until it is frothy and starts to stiffen a little. Then stir in the apples, sugar, and cinnamon.

To make the blintzes, take 1 rounded tablespoon of filling and place it in the center of each pancake. Fold the top edge to the center, covering the filling. Then fold in one side and then the other side and then fold it up, forming a square. Repeat with remaining filling and pancakes.

Preheat the oven to 350°F. Melt the pareve margarine and stir it together with the brown sugar. Arrange the blintzes on a greased baking pan and sprinkle them with the brown sugar mixture. Bake the blintzes until they are hot and bubbling, for about 15 minutes.

Blueberry Blintzes

Blueberry blintzes are one of my favorite things to eat for breakfast in the summertime. I like them best served sizzling hot straight from the pan, topped with sour cream, cinnamon, and sugar.

Makes 9 to 10 servings (2 per serving)

Batter

2 large eggs, lightly beaten

1 cup all-purpose flour

2 cups water

4 ounces (1 stick) pareve margarine, for greasing, divided

Filling

1½ cups blueberries

3 tablespoons granulated sugar, plus more for sprinkling

1 tablespoon cornstarch

⅛ teaspoon ground nutmeg

For the batter: Always crack your eggs individually into a small bowl to make sure they are okay. Pour them into a larger bowl and beat slightly. Then, add a little flour to the eggs and stir a little. Add a little flour alternately with a little water and continue stirring until a very thin smooth batter is formed. I find that sometimes it's easier to mix the batter with a spoon than a fork. Place a smooth dish towel on the table or counter.

Heat an 8-inch nonstick frying pan over medium heat. Measure 3 tablespoons of batter into a small dish. Take the pan off the heat (do not turn off the stove) and quickly grease the pan with a little pareve margarine. I use a piece of waxed paper or pastry brush to lightly coat the pan evenly. After greasing the pan, quickly pour in the batter. Tilt the pan so that the batter coats the bottom in an even, thin layer, returning the pan to the burner. Don't worry if the first few don't come out right. It's all about developing a partnership with the frying pan. Even the best of us do not succeed with the first ones. Cook until the pancake is dry and set at the edges and releases easily from the pan, 1 to 2 minutes. Flip the frying pan over onto the cloth dish towel, making sure to hit the pan against the counter top to help loosen the blintz, and let the blintz cool. Repeat with remaining batter, coating the pan with pareve margarine for each blintz. Be sure to stir the batter every time you measure it out because the flour and liquid tend to separate.

To make the filling, in a bowl, mix together the blueberries, sugar, cornstarch, and nutmeg.

To make the blintzes, take 1 rounded tablespoon of filling and place it in the center of each pancake. Fold the top edge to the center, covering the filling. Then fold in one side and then the other side and then fold it up, forming a square. Repeat with remaining filling and pancakes.

Preheat the oven to 350°F. Arrange the blintzes on a greased baking pan and sprinkle lightly with the granulated sugar. Bake the blintzes until they are hot and bubbling, about 15 minutes.

Blueberry Coffee Cake (Blueberry Buckle)

I like to make this coffee cake in the summer, when blueberries are in season. When you are hungry for a snack and want something sweet, it is just the thing with a cup of coffee or a glass of milk. You can also serve it for dessert with a little vanilla ice cream.

Makes 12 to 15 servings

Cake

4 tablespoons margarine

¾ cup granulated sugar

1 large egg

2 cups all-purpose flour

2 teaspoons baking powder

½ teaspoon kosher salt

½ cup milk

2 cups fresh blueberries

Topping

½ cup sugar

⅓ cup all-purpose flour

½ teaspoon cinnamon

4 tablespoons unsalted butter, softened

For the cake: Preheat the oven to 375°F. Grease a 9 x 9-inch baking pan.

In a large bowl, beat the margarine and the sugar with an electric mixer until it is nice and light and fluffy, about 2 minutes. Add the egg and beat well.

In another bowl, stir together the flour, baking powder, and salt. First, add a little flour mixture to the margarine mixture, then a little milk, then a little more flour, beating well after each addition. Gently blend in the blueberries. Spread the batter in the prepared pan.

For the topping: In a small bowl, mix together the sugar, flour, cinnamon, and butter until it is crumbly. Sprinkle the topping over the cake. Bake the cake for 45 to 50 minutes, until a toothpick inserted in the center comes out with a few crumbs attached.

yiddish word of the day ✡ **mishpokhe = family**

Lox and Cream Cheese Rollups

Lavash is a traditional flatbread from the Middle East. It's sort of like a pita with no pocket. You can find it in most grocery stores. In a pinch, substitute a whole wheat tortilla. Lox and cream cheese rollups are one of my favorites for any meal. The flavors are so delicious: the salty lox, creamy cheese, briny olives—and all the fresh, crunchy vegetables. Yum!

Makes 4 servings

8 tablespoons whipped cream cheese

4 round lavash breads

8 thin slices lox

12 medium black olives, pitted and halved

Coarsely chopped lettuce

Tomato slices

Cucumber slices

4 whole scallions, sliced diagonally

Schmear 2 tablespoons cream cheese over one side of each lavash bread. Place 2 slices of lox on top, and six of the olive haves. Fold the lavash breads over once by one-third, and fold in the sides. Next, add a layer of tomato and lettuce. Fold the lavash breads over again, then add a layer of cucumber and scallions. Fold the lavash breads once more, then cut each roll in half.

yiddish word of the day ✡ **bashert = meant to be**

The First Taste of Lox

In my family, lox is soul food. We consider it a staple and always have some tucked away in the refrigerator. When you top a plain bagel with cream cheese and lox, the results are like magic! Make rollups with cream cheese, lox, lettuce, tomato, and olives. Lox is so delicious, I can think of almost nothing better.

Before Zadie retired, I used to pack his lunch every day to take to work. One day I gave him a bagel with cream cheese and lox. One of his coworkers asked him, "What are you eating?"

"A bagel with lox," Zadie replied.

"What is lox?" asked the coworker.

Zadie explained that lox is smoked salmon, and it tastes especially terrific on a bagel with cream cheese. "You can buy it at Whitman's creamery," Zadie said. "Ask for a quarter pound of lox."

The coworker did just that. A few days later he said to Zadie, "Oh my goodness, how can you eat that lox stuff? It was one of the saltiest foods I've ever tasted!"

"What do you mean?" Zadie asked. "How did you eat it?"

"Well," said the coworker, "I took the whole quarter pound and put it on a bagel with cream cheese."

Zadie burst out laughing. "No wonder you couldn't eat it! A quarter pound of lox is enough for a whole family. You are only supposed to put one thin slice on your bagel."

To this day, we remember this story and have a good laugh. Imagine

Zadie with cup raised across from the coworker who ate the lox

eating a whole quarter pound of lox! The salty, briny flavor is quite strong and a little goes a very long way.

Today, you can buy many kinds of lox, including smoked salmon, called Nova, which is milder in flavor and not so salty. But back when I was growing up, there were just two kinds: one was pinkish red in color and the other was white. The white lox was the mildest of all. My mother used to fry the lox with eggs, onions, peppers, and tomatoes, which helped cut the salt and made a wonderful breakfast.

I remember when I was ten years old, going down to Mr. Whitman's store and buying lox. We used to call him Old Man Mr. Whitman. I loved to watch him work. He took the lox out of the case and put it on the counter. Then he used a very sharp knife to cut the lox paper thin. In those days, a quarter pound only cost thirteen cents!

Another breakfast treat I remember was coffee and milk. I think the fancy drinks at coffee shops are so funny! Why is a latte such a big deal? It is just coffee and milk. My mother made lattes almost every day for breakfast and we never had a gourmet name for them. To us, it was just called coffee and hot milk.

Here is how my mother did it. She took a small saucepan and poured in a cup of milk. Then she added three teaspoons of regular coffee and very slowly brought it to a boil. Then she took out a fine strainer and strained the coffee and milk into a cup. We all added sugar to it ourselves. It was so rich, thick, and delicious! Now in those days, there was no such thing as skim or low-fat milk. It was all 100 percent regular wholesome milk. So you can imagine the creamy flavor. Oh, it was such a beautiful hot drink for morning breakfast.

Cinnamon Rolls (Milchig Bulkelach)

These cinnamon rolls can seem like a lot of work, but they taste absolutely heavenly. I like to bake them for weekend breakfasts, and especially for Shabbos (Saturday) morning. There is nothing quite like the smell of cinnamon and sugar in the oven! I love raisins, but if you don't, just leave them out. Make an extra batch to keep in your freezer.

Makes 18 rolls

Dough

2 packages active dry yeast
(¼ ounce each)

¼ cup lukewarm water

1 cup milk

¼ cup vegetable oil, plus
more for brushing the dough

½ cup granulated sugar

1 teaspoon kosher salt

4 to 5 cups all-purpose flour

2 large eggs

1 teaspoon freshly grated
lemon zest

Filling

⅓ to ½ cup granulated sugar

1 teaspoon cinnamon

½ cup golden raisins
(optional)

For the dough: Combine the yeast with the water in small bowl. Stir it and then let it soften. In a small saucepan, scald the milk. Pour the milk into a large bowl and add the vegetable oil, sugar, and salt. Stir to combine, and let the mixture cool until it is lukewarm.

Add 2 cups of flour to the milk mixture and stir well. Add the eggs and lemon zest and mix well. Add the softened yeast and mix well. Add enough of the remaining flour to make a soft dough.

Dust your work surface with flour and turn the dough out onto it. Knead the dough until it is smooth and satiny, about 5 minutes. If it gets too sticky, add a little flour. Place the dough in a greased bowl and turn the dough once to grease both sides. Cover the bowl with plastic wrap or a dish towel and let the dough rise for about 2 hours, until it has doubled in size.

Meanwhile, **make the filling** and prepare the baking dishes. In a small bowl, mix together the sugar and cinnamon. Grease a 13 x 9-inch baking dish. Also grease an 8-inch round baking pan. This recipe sure makes a lot of cinnamon rolls!

yiddish word of the day ✡ **farmisht = mixed up**

Dust your work surface with flour again, and dust a rolling pin with flour. Roll the dough out into an 18 x 10-inch rectangle. With a pastry brush, brush the surface of the dough with vegetable oil. Sprinkle the dough evenly with the filling. Sprinkle with the raisins (if you are using them).

Starting with a long edge, roll the dough up into a log. Cut the log into eighteen slices. Place twelve of the slices in the 13 x 9-inch baking dish. Place the remaining six slices in the 8-inch round baking pan. Cover both with plastic wrap or dish towels and let them rise for 30 to 35 minutes, until they have doubled in size. Meanwhile, preheat the oven to 350°F.

Bake the cinnamon rolls for 25 to 30 minutes until they are golden-brown. Cool them for 5 minutes in the pans, then remove the rolls and let them cool completely on a wire rack.

The Catskills

My sister and her family lived in Brooklyn, New York. Since the summers are so hot there, every year they rented a bungalow upstate in the Catskills. My sister always invited Zadie and me and our children to join them. Who were we to say no? We went each summer for many, many years.

The bungalow my sister rented was part of what they called a bungalow colony. There were about a dozen bungalows in all. Each consisted of a kitchen and two bedrooms, plus a porch. Somehow there was enough room for all of us! Since it was warm, we often set up lounge chairs and beach chairs in the kitchen and on the porch to sleep. You might think the children would fight with each other in such close quarters, but in fact they had a ball playing and swimming.

One rainy day, all the children from the neighboring bungalows came over to play. Before I knew it there were about a dozen small children between the ages of seven and ten all playing in one room! Can you imagine? Later in the afternoon they all came out and it looked like clowns coming out of a tiny car at the circus.

While in the Catskills Bubbe and Zadie visit the historic Woodstock Landmark

Every morning and evening, we took advantage of what the resorts nearby had to offer. At the Concord Hotel, there was a fitness instructor who led games of Simon Says, which was a great way to get the children to exercise in the morning. I loved to take my children. They laughed and laughed.

In the evenings, we attended wonderful live shows put on by famous singers and comedians, like Jerry Lewis, Milton Berle, Buddy Hackett, and Jackie Mason. The entertainment was really tops. In those days, that part of the Catskills was known as the "Borscht Belt" because so many Jewish people vacationed there. It was a real hot spot. If a performer could make it there, they could make it anywhere.

And the food—my goodness, the food! There was so much it was unbelievable. For breakfast alone there were fresh juices, cereals, kippered herring with small, boiled potatoes, lox, pickled salmon, pickled herring, bagels and cream cheese, and tiny cinnamon rolls. There was no end, and if you wanted more, you could always ask for seconds. The waiters were like magicians—they never wrote down a thing, yet they always remembered your order perfectly, providing us with three meals a day, plus coffee and snacks at the evening shows.

Those summers at the Catskills, surrounded by my family, enjoying delicious food and top-notch entertainment, were some of the best times of my life. It makes me sad that so many of the resorts have closed. These days people go on faraway vacations and cruises. My hope and dream is that someday, someone will bring back the resorts in the Catskill Mountains to their former glory.

Appetizers & Salads

Old-fashioned Jewish appetizing stores are places where Jewish people traditionally went to buy dairy and pareve (neutral or kosher) foods like lox, whitefish, and pickled herring. There are still a few appetizing stores left, but today most of the foods can be found at the supermarket. (If you're keeping kosher just make sure to check the package.) I'm not quite sure why they were called "appetizing" stores, but it sure does make sense because they carried a large variety of appetizers and hors d'oeuvres in one central location.

I always have something to nibble on and am ready when I am expecting company. If my friends or family arrive at my house hungry I want to be able to feed them. In this chapter I'm going to show you how to make all kinds of delicious, classic Jewish appetizers like Chopped Chicken Liver, Chopped Herring, and Chopped Eggs and Onions. If you had a bubbe of your own, I'm sure my recipes will remind you of her food. And if you didn't, you're in for a treat! These dishes are going to become your favorites. They are so simple to prepare. Your guests will be amazed that you didn't spend all day in the kitchen.

In addition to the classic recipes, I'll also show you how to make some of my family's best-loved appetizers, like Potato-Wrapped Cocktail Franks and Mini Blintzes prepared with white sandwich bread. Both of those are extremely popular with the children!

Plus, there are some new recipes that I have picked up from friends and family over the years. I may be a traditional bubbe, but I love foods like hummus and puff pastry.

I'm sure you know that it's important to eat your greens, but I just had to say it anyway to remind you. Bubbes want to keep their grandchildren healthy! I always incorporate a green vegetable with every meal. Sometimes, that means having a salad. But salads don't have to be a plain mix of lettuce and tomatoes. There are so many different kinds. A centuries-old Jewish recipe is for Black Radish Salad flavored with a little chicken schmaltz. I also love cucumbers and scallions with fresh dill, and a big fruit salad with my delicious lime sauce. I'm also going to share with you my recipe for Charoset, which is a spread to put on matzo that is made from grated apples, cinnamon, honey, and sweet kosher wine. It is a very special dish that is always served as part of the Passover Seder.

Chopped Chicken Liver

Chopped chicken liver is one of the most famous and best-loved Jewish dishes. Few holiday meals are complete without it as an appetizer. Give my recipe a try. Once all the ingredients are cooked and puréed together in the food processor, it's so creamy and delicious! You can serve chopped chicken liver as a first course on a bed of lettuce garnished with sliced olives, cherry tomatoes, or whatever you have on hand, or as an hors d'oeuvre with rye bread, crackers, or bagel chips.

In this recipe I have included two large hard-boiled eggs, but for a healthier version, when I make this I would use three hard-boiled egg whites, which I have provided as an option. In addition normally you would use schmaltz (rendered chicken fat), but instead I have substituted it with sautéed onions with vegetable oil. If you choose to do it my way it will have great flavor and taste with the satisfaction in knowing that you made it in a healthier way than normally served.

Makes 6 to 8 appetizer servings

1 pound chicken livers

Kosher salt

2 tablespoons vegetable oil

1 large onion, diced

2 large hard-boiled eggs
  or 3 large hard-boiled
  egg whites

Pepper

Preheat the broiler and line a baking sheet with aluminum foil. Arrange a wire rack over the foil.

Rinse the chicken livers and pat them dry with paper towels. Clean the livers by trimming any visible fat or membranes. Arrange the livers in a single layer on the wire rack and sprinkle them on all sides with salt. Broil the livers for 3 to 5 minutes on each side, until they are cooked through and there are no traces of pink inside. Remove the livers from the broiler and set aside.

Heat the vegetable oil in a large frying pan over medium heat. Add the onions and sauté until lightly browned, about 10 minutes. Remove the pan from the heat, add the livers, and let the livers and onions cool to room temperature together.

When the livers and onions have cooled, place them in a food processor and pulse until they are chopped fine. Add the hard-boiled eggs and pulse until the mixture is well combined and has a paste consistency.

Transfer the liver mixture to a bowl and season to taste with salt and pepper. If the liver looks dry, add a teaspoon or two of vegetable oil. Cover the bowl with plastic wrap and refrigerate the liver for at least 2 hours, to allow the flavors to blend. Remove the chopped liver from the refrigerator 30 minutes before serving.

Mock Chopped Chicken Liver

In my family, it's very important that we all get together at least once or twice a year. All the aunts, uncles, cousins, and grandkids relax, swap stories, catch up, and share dishes that have been passed down for generations. At one such family meal, a family member brought mock chicken liver. All of us were fooled! I couldn't believe it was made with lentils. It tasted so rich and decadent. I just had to have the recipe.

Makes 6 to 8 servings

1 cup dried lentils

2 cups water

3 teaspoons pareve chicken-flavored seasoning

2 tablespoons vegetable oil

1 large onion, diced

¾ cup chopped walnuts

2 large hard-boiled eggs or 3 large hard-boiled egg whites

Kosher salt and pepper

Place the lentils in a strainer and run under cold water. Give them a little stir to make sure they are all well rinsed. Pick through the lentils to make sure there are no stones or little bits of other stuff.

Place the lentils in a large saucepan and add water. Bring to a boil, then turn the heat down to low. Stir in the chicken-flavored seasoning. Cover the pot and continue to cook over low heat for 20 to 30 minutes, until the lentils are soft and the water is absorbed. If the water is all absorbed but the lentils aren't tender, add a little bit more water and continue to cook until the lentils are done.

Heat a frying pan over medium heat. Add the vegetable oil and the onions and cook, stirring a little, until the onions are lightly browned, about 10 minutes. Remove the pan from the heat and set aside.

Place the walnuts in a food processor and process until they are finely ground. Add the hard-boiled eggs, the onions, and the lentils. Process until everything is thoroughly mixed and smooth. Transfer the lentil mixture to a large bowl and season with salt and pepper. Mix everything together well with a spoon, cover the bowl with plastic wrap, and refrigerate for several hours. Take the bowl out of the refrigerator about 30 minutes before serving.

yiddish word of the day ✡ **nokhamol** = again

Chopped Eggs and Onions

This recipe for chopped eggs and onions is so easy to make—especially now that most people have a food processor in their kitchen! It's wonderful served as an appetizer before dinner when you have company, or for a light lunch. Some versions of this dish are made with schmaltz (rendered chicken fat), but when I want to make the dish pareve I use olive oil. It's so much healthier!

 or

Makes 4 to 6 servings

4 tablespoons mild olive oil or rendered chicken fat (see Schmaltz and Gribenes, page 101)

⅓ cup thinly sliced onions

4 large hard-boiled eggs

⅓ cup diced onions

Kosher salt and pepper

Lettuce leaves and tomato slices for serving

Heat the oil in a large skillet over medium heat. Add the sliced onions and sauté until they are lightly browned. Watch carefully so that the onions don't burn. Scrape the onions into a bowl and let them cool a little bit.

When the cooked onions have cooled, place them in a food processor and pulse until they are roughly chopped. Add the eggs and the raw, chopped onions and process until the mixture is coarsely combined. Taste the eggs and season them with salt and pepper. If they seem a little dry, add another drop or two of olive oil. Chill the eggs in the refrigerator. Serve with lettuce and tomato slices.

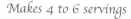

yiddish word of the day ✡ **a bi gezunt** = so long as you're healthy (like saying "be well")

Salmon Puff Pastry Bites

These appetizers look so fancy when you arrange them on a pretty platter. No one has to know that you made the salmon in advance, or that the puff pastry shells are from the grocery store. With children and grandchildren running around, I gave up trying to make everything from scratch a long time ago. Poaching the salmon keeps it moist and flavorful, and the dill adds a light, fresh flavor.

Makes 15 servings

1 (1-pound) salmon fillet, skinned

1 medium onion, sliced

½ stalk of celery, diced

Pinch of kosher salt

Pepper

¾ to 1 cup water

1 tablespoon cornstarch

1 package mini puff pastry shells, prepared according to package instructions just before serving

Handful chopped fresh dill

Place the salmon, onions, celery, salt, and pepper in a large pot and add the water (just enough to cover the fish). Bring the pot to a simmer over medium heat, and simmer for about 15 minutes, until the salmon is cooked.

Carefully take the salmon out of the pot and place it in a large bowl. (Don't pour out the cooking liquid! You'll need it in a minute.) Mix the cornstarch with 2 tablespoons of water and stir until smooth. Add the cornstarch mixture to the pot with the salmon cooking liquid. Stir well and bring the pot back to a boil just for a minute. Strain the cooking liquid and pour carefully over the salmon in the bowl. Let it cool slightly, and then refrigerate for several hours, until the liquid turns into a thick jelly.

Prepare the puff pastry shells just before serving so that they don't get soggy. Cut the salmon into one-inch chunks. Fit each chunk into a pastry shell bottom and add a little cold jelly broth and a pinch of dill. Serve at room temperature.

yiddish word of the day ✡ **sheyn = beautiful, pretty**

Chopped Herring

There are so many recipes for herring. You can pickle herring, bake it, fry it, or smother it with sour cream. It has a strong salty flavor, but don't be intimidated. Try it! You'll like it—especially if you prepare this recipe. The apple and the green pepper make it taste light and fresh. For a healthier version, you can use three hard-boiled egg whites in place of the whole hard-boiled eggs. I like to serve chopped herring spooned on top of rye or pumpernickel toast cut into triangles.

Makes 8 to 10 servings

1 (16-ounce) jar herring in wine sauce

2 slices challah or white bread, crusts removed, torn into pieces

2 large hard-boiled eggs or three large hard-boiled egg whites

1 large onion, peeled and diced

1 medium apple, peeled, cored, and cut into cubes

½ small green bell pepper, diced (optional)

1 tablespoon sugar, or more to taste

2 tablespoons cider vinegar or white vinegar, or more to taste

Drain the jar of herring over the sink and place the fish in the food processor. Pulse two or three times, just to break up the pieces. Add the bread, hard-boiled eggs, onions, apple, and green pepper (if you're using it) and pulse until the mixture is chopped fine.

Scoop the herring mixture into a large bowl and stir in the sugar and the vinegar. Do this gently so that you don't mash up the fish too much! Take a little taste and add another pinch of sugar or drop of vinegar, if needed. Cover the herring and refrigerate for several hours to allow the flavors to blend.

yiddish word of the day ✡ **haynt = today**

Yom Kippur Traditions, New and Old

Yom Kippur, the Jewish day of atonement, is the holiest day of the year. We fast for a full day, from sundown to about an hour after sundown the next day. The day before Yom Kippur is one of the most hectic days of the year! There is so much cooking to be done in preparation for the break-the-fast meal the following evening.

Zadie in uniform in front of his parents' home on leave during World War II

Bubbe and Zadie's engagement party in 1946

The last meal before beginning the fast is always a big one. I like to serve all my favorites: the traditional large round loaf of challah (which is served only during the high holy days), gefilte fish, chicken soup with kreplach or noodles, roast chicken, rice, a green vegetable, and tea and honey cake for dessert. It's a feast, but you need to store up energy for the long day ahead. The following day during services at the synagogue, occasionally there would be one person who became overwhelmed with all the activity, the heat, and the lack of food. Then someone would have to run to the kitchen to get smelling salts to wave under their nose. I'm proud to say that I have never passed out during Yom Kippur!

During the last half-hour of services at synagogue, everyone is watching the clock. As soon as the shofar (an instrument made out of a ram's horn) is blown we wish each other a "happy new year" and then hurry home to eat. Ever since I can remember, the first thing my family has is "tshaynik milk," which is boiled water with milk and sugar. The tshaynik milk, along with some challah and butter, is so soothing—just the thing to help our stomachs get reacquainted with eating. Then we move on to other foods, like delicious pickled herring, followed by drinking some hot water, and then some hot chicken soup.

Now that I'm a bubbe and getting on in years, fasting is a little bit exhausting. It's hard to believe that when I was young I used to go out dancing after Yom Kippur! Somehow at that age nothing gets to you. You have all the energy in the world. My friends and I used to go to a break-the-fast dance sponsored by the B'nai Brith Girls and the AZA Boys Organization, which we all belonged to. And if there wasn't a dance, well, we would go to the theater for a movie or vaudeville. It was always a really social time for the fellows and girls to mingle and enjoy each other's company.

One of my favorite Yom Kippur traditions took place late in the afternoon, just when everyone is beginning to feel especially restless, hungry, and tired. The young people would walk around the neighborhood and visit the other synagogues. There were about six in our town, and we stopped in to each, one after the other. One year, when I was twenty years old, during these visits I bumped into Zadie, whom I hadn't seen in a long time. He had been in the service for almost four years during World War II. "Boy, you've grown up," he said. And wouldn't you know it, that was the start of a beautiful relationship.

Israeli Herring

I never had herring prepared this way until my friend made this dish. I thought it was so wonderful that I just had to have her recipe. The tomato paste binds the other ingredients together and gives it a slightly sweet flavor and a rosy color. I like to serve this on rye bread or crackers. Best of all, you can make it a couple of days in advance.

Makes 15 to 20 servings

1 (32-ounce) jar herring in wine sauce

¼ cup cider vinegar

¼ cup vegetable oil

¼ cup sugar

2 (6-ounce) cans tomato paste

2 apples, peeled, cored, and diced

2 large onions, peeled and diced

Drain the herring over the sink and pat the fish dry with paper towels. Cut the herring into small, bite-size pieces and place them in a large bowl. In another bowl, mix together the cider vinegar, vegetable oil, sugar, and tomato paste. Stir in the apples and onions. Pour the mixture over the herring and stir well to blend. Cover the herring and refrigerate until it is chilled.

yiddish word of the day ✡ **khaver = friend**

Pickled Salmon

There is nothing like this classic dish to bring back memories of being at the Catskills. Typically I would serve this as a part of a special Sunday morning breakfast or brunch. The sour cream sauce makes this recipe dairy but it is still enjoyable even without the sauce should you want to make it pareve.

 P or **D**

Makes 8 to 10 servings

¾ teaspoon kosher salt

⅔ cup sugar

1 cup white vinegar

½ cup water

1½ pounds fresh salmon filet, skin removed

2 large onions sliced about ¼ inch thick

1 tablespoon plus 1 teaspoon pickling spice

5 whole bay leaves

Sour Cream Sauce

1 tablespoon marinade

¼ cup sour cream

In small saucepan combine the salt, sugar, vinegar, and water. Bring to a boil and let completely cool. Cut salmon into small pieces about 1½ x 1½ inches. Separate the onion slices into rings. In a large bowl layer salmon pieces, then sprinkle with pickling spice and 2 bay leaves and then a layer of onions and repeat these layers until all ingredients have been used. Pour cold marinade over all and cover with plastic wrap. Place in the refrigerator to marinate for four days. On the third day gently stir all of the ingredients so they will mix well with the marinade. The pickled salmon is ready to eat on the fourth day and will keep in the refrigerator for 7 to 10 days.

To **make the sauce,** remove the salmon and combine the marinade and sour cream in a glass or nonreactive metal bowl and mix well. It is best to mix the sauce several hours before serving so that it will not take away from the taste of the pickled salmon. Serve the sauce with the salmon.

Note: If you have to skin the salmon yourself, cut it into 1½-inch lengths and with a knife against the skin slowly separate the salmon from the skin. Make sure to buy a good-quality pickling spice so that spices will not be extremely tiny and adhere to the salmon.

yiddish word of the day ✡ **fendle = saucepan**

Charoset

Charoset is a sweet apple relish made with walnuts and kosher wine. It is one of the five foods of the Passover Seder plate, along with parsley dipped in salt water, an egg, a shank bone, and bitter herbs (usually horseradish). Charoset is meant to symbolize the mortar and bricks enslaved Jews in Egypt were forced to make.

Children especially love charoset—the crunchy apples and walnuts, the sweet grape wine, and the cinnamon and sugar make it taste almost like dessert. It is delicious when spooned over matzo.

Makes 6 to 8 servings

3 large peeled tart apples

1 cup finely chopped walnuts

½ to ¾ teaspoon cinnamon

1 to 2 teaspoons sugar or honey

2 to 4 tablespoons sweet kosher Concord grape wine

Peel the apples and grate them on the large holes of a box grater. Place them in a bowl. Add the walnuts, ½ teaspoon of cinnamon, and 1 teaspoon of sugar. Mix everything together with a large spoon. Add just enough wine to moisten and bind the mixture together. Taste the charoset and add more cinnamon, sugar, or wine, if desired.

---

yiddish word of the day ✡ **kanoble = garlic**

Potato-Wrapped Cocktail Franks

This recipe is such a crowd pleaser. Who wouldn't love miniature hot dogs? This would be a great dish to serve when you are having friends over to watch a baseball game on TV. Just add a bowl of salted peanuts and ice-cold sodas.

Makes 6 to 10 servings

2 large baking potatoes

2 tablespoons pareve margarine

1 large egg, lightly beaten

Kosher salt and pepper

12 cocktail franks or 6 regular-size hot dogs

¾ cup crushed cornflakes

Pinch of paprika

Spicy brown mustard, for serving

Sweet and sour sauce, for serving

Peel the potatoes and cut them into large cubes. Place the cubes in a large pot and add just enough water to cover them. Bring the pot to a boil, then turn the heat down to a simmer and cook for 10 to 15 minutes, until the potatoes are tender. Drain the potatoes and mash them well with a large fork.

Let the potatoes cool a little bit, then stir in the margarine, beaten egg, and a pinch of salt and pepper. Set the potato mixture aside.

Bring another pot of water to boil and add the cocktail franks or hot dogs. Boil for 3 or 4 minutes until the franks are hot. Place them on a plate. If you are using regular-size hot dogs, cut them in half across the middle.

Preheat the oven to 350°F. Mix the cornflakes and paprika on a plate. Using your hands, coat each cocktail frank or hot dog half with the potato mixture, shaping each one into a log. Roll each "log" in the cornflake crumbs and put them on a baking sheet. Bake the franks for 40 to 50 minutes, until they are nice and crispy. Serve them hot, with bowls of mustard and sweet and sour sauce for dipping.

yiddish word of the day ✡ **shlep = carry, pull**

Two Bulkie Rolls, Three Frankfurters, and a Snowstorm

Many years ago, there was a very big snowstorm in the Northeast. I was one of the lucky ones who was able to leave work early. Many of my coworkers got stuck at the office for two or three nights!

When we awoke the morning after the storm, the snow was so high it covered the doors and windows. We went out to shovel the snow and it was taller than my children. We couldn't even see the storefronts! It was just my luck that I was supposed to do the shopping the next day. We had very little food in the house. We were stuck for almost a week. After several days, supplies were really running low. All I had left were two bulkie rolls and three frankfurters. Bulkie rolls are similar to kaiser rolls. If you haven't had the opportunity to experience a bulkie roll, then you have to make a trip to New England where they are readily available.

What could I do? Normally, the children ate two frankfurters apiece. I decided the best thing to do was to cut each frankfurter in half the long way. Then I made two sandwiches with one and a half frankfurters in each. I topped each one with mustard, relish, and chopped onions. The kids loved them! To this day, that's how I make frankfurters. I call them "Hot Dog and a Half Sandwiches."

About three years ago, there was another terrible storm. This time it was an ice storm. It was really something. All the power went out. We had no electricity, and it was the middle of winter. The first night we thought,

Zadie shoveling snow during the northeast blizzard of 1978

"Oh, we'll just pile on the blankets and it will be all right." But when we got up in the morning the house was freezing—really dangerously cold. Only one radio station was working. The newscaster said it would be several days before the power came back on.

We started calling hotels. Where could we stay? All the hotels were booked with other people who had the same idea. Finally, we were able to find a room with a kitchen fifty miles away. So my daughter and her children and Zadie and I packed the necessary supplies in the car. I took my crock pot, and I looked in the freezer. What foods could I take along? What would be easy to prepare? I grabbed a couple of packages of frankfurters, a couple of packages of bulkie rolls, and some cans of fruit. Then we jumped in the car and drove through the icy streets all the way to the hotel.

It took a long time to get there, and by that time everyone was starving. I was able to get the crock pot going, and again I made Hot Dog and a Half Sandwiches. They tasted so good. Can you imagine? Our first hot meal when we were so hungry.

It was more than a week before the power finally came back on at our house. The experience really helped me to appreciate the modern conveniences (like electric can openers) and warmth that we so often take for granted.

Mini Blintzes

I love blintzes, but sometimes I'm too busy to make the batter. That's why I came up with this recipe, which uses plain white sandwich bread! It's a family favorite, and will appeal to anyone with a sweet tooth. I often serve mini blintzes as an hors d'oeuvre. But beware—the gooey cream cheese and buttery, toasty bread is hard to resist. Don't put out too many or your guests might spoil their appetites for the main course!

Makes 10 to 12 servings (2 per serving)

½ cup sugar

1½ teaspoons cinnamon

1 loaf sliced white bread

1 (12-ounce) package cream cheese, softened

4 ounces (1 stick) margarine or butter, melted

Preheat the oven to 350°F.

Mix the sugar and cinnamon together in a small bowl. Cut the crusts off each slice of bread. Working with one piece of bread at a time, roll the bread out with a rolling pin so that it is flat and thin. Schmear each slice with a thin layer of cream cheese. With the long side of the bread facing you, roll each slice up like a jelly roll, forming little logs. Cut each log in half, roll them in the melted butter, and sprinkle them with cinnamon and sugar. Place them in a baking dish, making sure that they don't touch each other. Bake the blintzes for 15 minutes, until they are golden-brown and hot.

yiddish word of the day ✡ **tam or taam = taste**

Hummus

Hummus is a staple food in many Mediterranean countries, including Israel. Of course you can buy hummus at any supermarket, but homemade versions taste so much better, and it couldn't be easier to make—just put everything in the food processor or blender! I like to spread my hummus on pita bread. I also use it in sandwiches. Leftover hummus will keep well in your refrigerator for up to five days.

Makes 6 to 8 servings

1 (14-ounce) can chickpeas, rinsed and drained

3 garlic cloves, cut into quarters

1 tablespoon lemon juice

¼ cup tahini (sesame paste)

¼ teaspoon kosher salt

⅛ teaspoon pepper

¼ cup boiling water

Place the chickpeas, garlic, lemon juice, tahini, salt, and pepper in a blender or a food processor. Blend or process until the mixture forms a smooth paste. Gradually add the water, 1 or 2 tablespoons at a time, and blend until the mixture is smooth (you may not need all the water). Place the hummus in a bowl and refrigerate until it is well chilled.

yiddish word of the day ✡ **ponem = face**

Half-Sour Pickles

No sandwich would be complete without a pickle! The crunchy, salty, sour flavors of my easy homemade version are a perfect accompaniment to pastrami, corned beef, and even tuna fish. If you don't already have a jar of pickling spice, you can find it in most supermarkets, on the shelf with the other cooking spices.

Makes 18 to 24 servings

18 to 24 Kirby cucumbers (pickling cucumbers)

½ bunch fresh dill

½ cup white vinegar

¼ cup kosher salt

4 garlic cloves, peeled and crushed

1 tablespoon pickling spice

Wash and dry the cucumbers and place them in a 1-gallon glass jar with a tight-fitting lid. Add the dill, vinegar, salt, garlic, and pickling spice. Fill the jar with lukewarm water, leaving ½ inch of space at the top. Place a piece of plastic wrap folded over twice over the mouth of the jar and screw on the lid tightly. Turn the jar over and shake it gently, just to mix the spices and everything together. You may be temped to eat them right away, but don't! Leave the pickles alone in a cool, dry place for four or five days to let the flavors develop. Taste one pickle to see if it is done enough. If not, let them sit for another day or two. When the pickles are ready, store them in the refrigerator until you are ready to serve them.

yiddish word of the day ✡ **zoyer** = sour

Sour Green Tomatoes

This is a really old-fashioned recipe! My mother used to make pickled green tomatoes this way, and they were so tangy and irresistible. To make my sour green tomatoes you will need a large round wooden board to go inside the container over the tomatoes and a clean, heavy rock from the backyard. You also need patience—the tomatoes can take from eight to fourteen days to pickle.

Makes 25 to 30 servings

25 to 30 green tomatoes

½ cup kosher salt

2 quarts of water

¾ cup white vinegar

5 garlic cloves, peeled and crushed

1 tablespoon pickling spice

½ bunch fresh dill

Wash the tomatoes and place them in a large, heavy, nonreactive pot (ceramic or stainless steel). Combine the salt with the water in a medium saucepan and bring to a boil. Boil until the salt has dissolved, then take the saucepan off the heat and let it cool.

When the salt water has cooled, stir in the vinegar, garlic, and pickling spice. Pour the mixture over the tomatoes and add the dill. The brine should cover the tomatoes completely. If it doesn't, add a little more water and salt.

Place the wooden board on top of the tomatoes and place the rock on top of the board to secure it. Cover the pot with plastic wrap. Put the pot in a cool, dry place and let it sit for four or five days.

Remove the rock and board and carefully stir the tomatoes with your hand. Check to see if the tomatoes have pickled enough— their color should be slightly dulled, and they should taste sour. If they are not ready let them sit for two or three more days.

When the tomatoes are pickled transfer them to glass jars. Strain the brine and pour it over the tomatoes. Cover the mouth of each jar with plastic wrap and then screw on the lid. Store the tomatoes in the refrigerator.

yiddish word of the day ✡ **muter = mother**

Lime-Laced Fruit Salad

If you're planning to make this fruit salad but your nectarines or peaches are too hard, here is a good trick: put them in a paper bag overnight. This speeds up the ripening process. My favorite part of this salad is the juicy, sweet fresh cherries. I just love cherries—I eat them like peanuts! My lime juice dressing makes this recipe just a little different, and a little more special.

Makes 10 to 12 servings

½ cup freshly squeezed lime juice (2 or 3 limes)

½ cup granulated sugar

½ cup water

1 large banana, peeled and sliced

2 large unpeeled nectarines or peaches, sliced

1 pint strawberries, trimmed and halved

1 cup seedless red or green grapes

1 cup cubed or balled watermelon

1 pint blueberries, reserve ½ cup for garnish

1 kiwi, peeled and sliced crosswise into rounds

12 Bing cherries, with stems

Combine the lime juice and sugar in a small bowl. Add water and stir until the sugar is dissolved. Add the banana slices. This keeps them from turning brown.

Strain out the banana slices (but don't throw out the lime juice mixture!) and arrange them around the bottom and sides of a glass serving bowl. Add the nectarine slices, strawberries, grapes, watermelon, and blueberries. Arrange the kiwi slices and the cherries over the top of the salad and pour the reserved lime juice mixture over the top. Sprinkle the reserved blueberries on top for a garnish. Covered tightly, this will keep in the refrigerator for three days.

yiddish word of the day ✡ **zeygerr = clock**

Ritach mit Schmaltz (Black Radish Salad)

This is a very, very old recipe. In Egypt they grew and ate radish salads like this one hundreds of years ago. Talk about time-tested! Black radishes are the size of beets. They get their name from their dark outside, but the flesh inside is actually white. To make the dish pareve use vegetable oil instead of schmaltz. Look for them starting in the early fall, when they come into season. This salad is traditionally served as an appetizer before a meal of chicken or beef.

 or

Makes 2 to 3 servings

1 black radish, peeled

1 medium onion

1 teaspoon rendered chicken fat (see Schmaltz and Gribenes, page 101) or vegetable oil

Kosher salt and pepper

Using the large grater holes, grate the radish into a bowl. Peel the onion and cut it crosswise into thin slices. Pull the slices apart into rings. Add the onions to the bowl with the radish. Add the chicken fat or vegetable oil and toss to mix well. Season the salad with salt and pepper.

yiddish word of the day ✡ **retekh = radish**

Cucumber and Scallion Salad with Fresh Dill

This is a light, refreshing salad that I love to serve with beef pot roast or chicken. The tangy vinegar and fresh dill add so much flavor and are a nice contrast to cut the richness of meat dishes. It is important to let the salad chill for several hours in the refrigerator before serving, so that the flavors can blend.

Makes 4 to 6 servings

3 cucumbers, peeled and thinly sliced crosswise

1½ teaspoons kosher salt

5 tablespoons white vinegar

⅛ teaspoon pepper

5 teaspoons granulated sugar, or more to taste

2 tablespoons water

3 whole small scallions, thinly sliced

2 tablespoons chopped fresh dill

Place the cucumber slices in a bowl and sprinkle them with the salt. Set them aside for 20 minutes. In a small bowl, combine the vinegar, pepper, sugar, and water. Mix well until the sugar is dissolved. Add the scallions and dill to the cucumbers. Pour the vinegar mixture over the cucumbers and toss well to combine. Chill for several hours before serving.

Homemade Horseradish

Horseradish is one of the bitter herbs included on the Passover Seder plate. When I was a little girl, it was my job to grate it. Let me tell you, fresh horseradish root sure can clear the sinuses! I would attach the hand grinder to the side of the seat of a wooden chair on our back porch. Then I would place the pieces of root in the grinder, turn the handle, and in this way grind the root. Being outside made the fumes a little more tolerable, but still I had to turn my face to the side as I worked. One whiff and whoa!

Even though it is quite strong, freshly grated horseradish makes a delicious condiment for gefilte fish, boiled chicken, or boiled meats. My recipe, which includes beets, vinegar, and a pinch of sugar, tastes so much better than the horseradish you can buy in jars at the supermarket.

Make sure you prepare this recipe in a well-ventilated area, and don't forget to turn your face when you take the cover off your food processor! It is strongest right after it is made, and mellows a bit after a few days in the refrigerator.

Makes about 2 cups

1 pound fresh horseradish root

3 medium beets

¼ cup white or cider vinegar

1 teaspoon kosher salt

1 teaspoon sugar

Give the horseradish root a good scrub in the sink. Peel the horseradish root, place it in a bowl of cold water, and let it soak for 20 minutes. Next, cut the horseradish root into slices about 1 inch thick. Peel the beets and cut them into 1-inch cubes.

Make sure your food processor is fitted with the grating attachment, then grate the horseradish root and beets.

Place the grated horseradish root and beets into a large bowl and add the vinegar, salt, and sugar. Mix everything together well. Stick a fork in and give it a taste. Adjust the seasoning with a bit more vinegar, salt, sugar, or water if necessary.

Transfer the horseradish to jars. Store them in the refrigerator.

yiddish word of the day ✡ **zeml** = bakery roll

Soups & Sandwiches

Steaming bowls of soup are part of just about every cuisine in the world, and with good reason. Soup is easy and economical to make, and so comforting to eat! Of course, of all the soups out there none are as soothing or healing as Jewish chicken soup with matzo balls. My recipe is not only delicious, it will also cure whatever ails you—and that's a bubbe guarantee! I learned to make it from my mother. Every week she and our neighbor bought one chicken to share. Each family got half a chicken. My mother added lima beans to the pot to stretch her soup. Times were tough but we got by and ate well, and no one was hungry. That's the great thing about soup—it's very cost-effective. The ingredients are inexpensive and one large pot can be enough to feed a family for days.

Soup is also so simple to make. For the most part, you just throw a bunch of vegetables and beef or chicken into a pot with some stock and let it bubble away. If you have some rice or noodles, you can add that, too. What could be easier? If you're just learning how to cook, preparing a few soup recipes from this chapter is a great place to start. I've included all my favorites. Some are great for the cold, winter months, like Beef Vegetable Soup, Meat Cabbage Borscht, and Fish Chowder. Others are perfect for summer, like my Cold Spinach Soup and Cold Beet Borscht. Soup is also a great dish to make ahead. I just love things that I can prepare and freeze. That way I always know I have a nutritious dinner on hand.

I have been making soup for my family for longer than I can remember! Over the years I've come up with a few tricks and tips. Here they are. First, when you are making chicken stock, it can be hard to skim all the fat off the surface. Sometimes I put the whole pot in the refrigerator for a few hours. All the fat rises up and congeals at the top, and it's easy to scrape off. Other times, if I'm in a hurry, I gently place a paper towel over the surface of my stock for just a few seconds. It absorbs most of the fat quickly. Second, bouillon cubes are a great way to add a little bit of extra flavor. If your soup tastes a bit bland add a cube to the pot. Lastly, experiment with vegetables! Most soup recipes are very adaptable. You can use my recipes as a starting point to create your own delicious renditions.

Sometimes soup is a meal on its own, but sometimes you need a little something else to go along with it. What goes better with soup than sandwiches? Just in case you're still hungry I've shared some of my family's favorite sandwich recipes, including a simple Tomato, Lettuce, and Onion Sandwich, an Eggless Egg Salad Sandwich made with tofu (yes, even bubbes eat tofu these days!), and my famous Bubbe's Burgers, which are just about my favorite thing when served on a bulkie roll with lots of ketchup and pickles.

Chicken Soup with Matzo Balls

I don't think there is a single food in the world more comforting than a steaming bowl of chicken soup with light, fluffy matzo balls—I always say it's like Jewish penicillin! I learned how to make this soup by watching my mother. Sometimes I like to add a chicken bouillon cube to enhance the flavors, which you can do if you like. This soup is a great way to start a hearty winter's meal. You can store leftovers in the freezer for up to three months, so don't be afraid to make a big batch.

Makes 6 servings

4 chicken leg quarters

6 cups cold water

2 stalks of celery with leaves, cut into thirds

1 medium onion, halved

1 large peeled carrot, cut crosswise into thirds

1 small peeled parsnip, cut crosswise into thirds

5 sprigs of fresh parsley or dill

1 chicken bouillon cube, or kosher salt to taste

1 box matzo ball mix

Using a sharp knife or kitchen sheers cut the extra fat from the chicken quarters—but be sure to leave the skin on for flavor. Rinse the chicken with cold water, then place it in a bowl and add enough boiling water to cover and then drain water. This makes it easier to remove any pin feathers. Rinse the chicken with cold water again. Place the chicken in a large pot and add 6 cups cold water. Bring the water to a boil, then lower the heat to a simmer. Skim any foam from the surface with a large spoon. Simmer the chicken for 1 hour. Add the celery, onion, carrot, parsnip, parsley, and bouillon to the pot. Continue to simmer for 30 minutes to 1 hour more, until the chicken meat is falling off the bones and the carrots are fork-tender.

Take the carrots and the chicken out of the pot gently with a large spoon and place it on a large plate to cool. Strain the soup into a large bowl. Throw away all the other vegetables and herbs. Cover the plate with plastic wrap and place it in the refrigerator for another use.

yiddish word of the day ✡ **kneydlach = dumpling**

When the soup has cooled, cover it with plastic wrap, too, and place it in the refrigerator. Chill the soup overnight. The next day, skim away the fat that has collected at the surface of the soup.

Prepare the matzo balls according to the package instructions. Reheat the soup over medium heat until it is piping hot. Ladle the soup into bowls and add a matzo ball (or two or three!) to each bowl before serving.

Note: You can add the chicken and carrots to the soup if you like or serve the carrots as a side dish and use the leftover chicken in my recipe for Tasty Soup Chicken (page 108) Instead of matzo balls, you can also add fine noodles or rice.

The Healing Powers of a Bubbe

I am a modern woman (I have my own Internet TV show for goodness sake!). So of course I believe in contemporary science and medicine. When my children or grand-children got sick, the first place we always went was to the doctor's office. But the second place was the butcher, where I would buy a nice, fat, kosher chicken. Antibiotics are all well and good, but any true bubbe knows that nothing cures an illness better than homemade chicken soup!

Even though the ingredients are almost always the same—chicken, celery, onions, carrots, a handful of fresh herbs, and some broth—no two bubbe's versions of chicken soup taste exactly alike. I have been making my soup for as long as I can remember. I don't even look at the recipe anymore. I know it by heart. I learned from watching my mother make her chicken soup, and she learned from watching her mother. When I start chopping vegetables, simmering chicken quarters, and shaping matzo balls, something magical happens. It's as if all the love and good wishes I have for my family and friends get tossed into the pot along with the other ingredients!

When I serve up steaming bowls of soup filled with tender carrots, big chunks of flavorful chicken, and fluffy matzo balls, I know that no cold or flu stands a chance. Sometimes when people get sick they lose their appetites. But "I'm not hungry" are a bubbe's least favorite words to hear. My chicken soup is like a secret weapon—it is so delicious and nourishing you can't help but slurp down whole bowlfuls, even when you have no appetite at all.

But the healing powers of a bubbe don't just stop at chicken soup. Most bubbes have at least one or two other recipes they swear will cure just about any ailment. I'm going to share mine with you. Try it the next time you have a cough or the sniffles. It will instantly make you feel ten times better.

The recipe is for a drink called gogul mogul. If you have a bubbe of your own you might have heard of it, or even had it when you were sick. The roots of gogul mogul lie in the Russian Jewish shtetls. Gogul mogul was commonly given to anyone with a sore throat, the flu, or just about anything else. It is so soothing that right from the very first sip you feel like you are on the mend.

There are many different recipes for gogul mogul. Some call for alcohol like brandy or rum. Others involve citrus juice, nutmeg, or cinnamon. My version is a simple classic that is easy to prepare with ingredients you are guaranteed to have on hand. All you need is an egg yolk, a little bit of sugar or honey, some milk, and a few drops of vanilla extract. Heat everything up together and yum! It is a drink that is not only nourishing and healing, but also incredibly delicious. Try it the next time you are feeling under the weather. I promise it will transform you into a new person!

Gogul Mogul

Makes 1 drink

1 large egg yolk

2 teaspoons sugar or honey

1 cup milk

A few drops vanilla extract

Place the egg yolk and the sugar or honey in a coffee mug. Mix them together with a spoon until they are well combined. In a small saucepan, heat the milk over medium heat until it is just barely simmering. Be careful not to burn it! Pour the milk into the mug a little at a time. It's important to stir constantly so that the egg yolk doesn't curdle. Add a few drops of vanilla extract and stir to combine.

Shirley Temple

Mention the name "Shirley Temple," and most people think of a sugary beverage made with ginger ale and maraschino cherries. But it makes me think of soup! Whenever my mother prepared her chicken vegetable soup, she would sing Shirley's song "Animal Crackers in My Soup." It went like this:

> Animal crackers in my soup
> Monkeys and rabbits loop the loop,
> Gosh, oh gee, but I have fun,
> Swallowin' animals one by one.

Oh, I loved Shirley Temple so much when I was a girl! I wanted to be just like her. I was jealous of my sister, who had curly hair that she could style like Shirley's. I was one of the unfortunate girls who had hair as straight as a pin.

There was a children's shop in town that carried a line of dresses modeled after the ones that Shirley wore. Two times a year we got new clothes. One time was in the spring, for Passover. Even though my parents were of limited means, they always bought me a Shirley Temple dress with little patent leather shoes, white gloves, and a straw hat to go with it. To this day I can remember one dress in particular: it was light yellow, with little brown polka dots and a little collar, and short sleeves.

Bubbe with her most favorite doll

My friends would come to my house to play with my Shirley Temple paper dolls. Every time the young actress made a new movie there was a new paper doll book. Each book cost about $1, which is probably about $5 or $10 today. The dolls were made out of cardboard and the dresses were paper with little tags on them. There were little hats and little shoes to match. We cut everything out with children's scissors. We played with the paper dolls so much that sometimes they wore out and ripped, and then we cried.

One of our neighbors, whose daughters were all grown, used to let me visit and play with her fancy doll. The doll's body was made of cloth stuffed with straw, but her feet, hands, and face were made of beautiful china. I had to be very careful when I played with her, because she was so delicate. One day I was playing and by accident she fell to the floor and her face broke into pieces. I was so upset! My neighbor was very nice about it, but to this day, I still remember it and feel bad.

I can't quite remember what happened after that, but I wouldn't be surprised if I went home crying, and my mother consoled me with a steaming bowl of chicken soup. In our family, chicken soup is the cure for just about everything!

Fish Chowder

When I was growing up, once a week a man would drive into the neighborhood and sell fish out of the back of his station wagon. Everyone came down to the street to buy mackerel, cod, and haddock. That night, my mother always prepared fish bulbe (fish and potatoes). Her version didn't have any milk, but I use one can of evaporated fat-free milk in mine. Not only does it make the chowder healthier, it gives it a rich, creamy taste. I like to serve this chowder with crackers or breadsticks.

Makes 8 to 10 servings

1 (1-pound) skinless haddock or cod fillet

2 cups water

3 large potatoes, peeled and cubed

2 medium carrots, peeled and diced

2 medium onions, halved and sliced into rounds

2 tablespoons margarine

1 (12-ounce) can evaporated fat-free milk

Kosher salt and pepper

Place the fish in a large pot. Add the water and bring to a boil. Turn the heat down to low and simmer the fish until it is just cooked, 8 to 10 minutes. It should be flaky and soft. Take the fish out of the pot and set it aside on a plate. (Leave the water in the pot.)

Add the potatoes, carrots, and onions to the pot, increase the heat to medium high, and cook until the vegetables are fork-tender, about 10 minutes.

Add the fish back to the pot, along with the margarine and the evaporated milk, and stir lightly. Heat the chowder until it is hot. Be careful and don't let it boil! Taste the chowder and season it with salt and pepper. Ladle the chowder into bowls and serve hot.

yiddish word of the day ✡ **bulbe = potato**

Cold Beet Borscht

Beets are common ingredients in Jewish cuisine. One of the best-known dishes with beets is borscht, a healthy soup with a brilliant ruby color. Borscht can be prepared many ways and served hot or cold. My favorite recipe uses canned beets and a few other pantry staples—it couldn't be easier to prepare! This soup makes a perfect summer lunch. I like to top it with a boiled potato or diced cucumber and a dollop of sour cream.

 or

Makes 4 to 5 servings

1 (15-ounce) can whole beets

3 cups water (see directions)

3 to 4 tablespoons lemon juice

¼ to ⅓ cup granulated sugar

1 teaspoon kosher salt

½ teaspoon onion powder

½ teaspoon garlic powder

Sour cream, for serving
 (optional)

Drain the liquid from the can of beets into a large saucepan, setting the beets aside. Fill the empty can one and a half times with water, which will equal 3 cups of water, and add it to the pan. Bring the mixture to a boil over medium heat.

Meanwhile, grate the beets on a box grater. Add them to the saucepan along with the lemon juice, ¼ cup sugar, salt, onion powder, and garlic powder. Cover the pan, lower the heat, and simmer the soup for 20 minutes. Taste the soup and add more sugar if needed.

Let the soup cool to room temperature, then pour it into a large bowl. Cover the bowl and chill the soup in the refrigerator until ready to serve. To serve, ladle the soup into bowls and top with a dollop of sour cream.

yiddish word of the day ✡ **tsuzamen = together**

Soup without Salt

On Sunday mornings when we were young my sister and I attended a history class at a Hebrew school where most of my friends went. My mother always walked with us to class and paid the teacher herself.

One Sunday I told my mother, "I'll take the money and give it to the teacher!"

"No no," my mother said. "You'll lose it."

"No I won't," I argued. "Please let me walk to Hebrew school by myself today."

Finally my mother relented and pressed a shiny silver half dollar into my palm. "Be very careful," she said. "Go straight to school and don't drop the money."

Well wouldn't you know it, not five minutes later the coin slipped through my fingers and plunged behind the back stairs of our house. I got down on my hands and knees and peeked through the cracks. I couldn't see anything. The money was lost.

Bubbe's children helping her mother, Molle, prepare for Passover in 1957

Bubbe made this Purim costume for her son, Ephraim. Here he is going to his Hebrew school party on Purim.

I was terrified of what my mother would say. I didn't know what to do. Fighting back tears, I knocked on the door of our neighbor, Mrs. Reed, who was wonderfully sweet—almost like a bubbe!

"Mrs. Reed," I sniffled. "I lost the money my mother gave me to pay my teacher at Hebrew school. She's going to be so mad at me! What do you think I should do?"

"Don't worry, I will give you the half dollar," Mrs. Reed said. She gave me a new coin and I hugged her and ran straight to school with my sister.

Of course, my mother found out about the incident not long after. She told me a story that I have never forgotten about the value of a penny:

> Once there was a wealthy Russian prince. He seemingly had everything in life, but his children were unruly. They had no sense of value or responsibility, and they never listened to him. One day, the prince asked his cook to prepare the children's soup without any salt at all. When the children sat down to dinner they tasted the soup and immediately began to complain about the taste. "This soup has no flavor!" they cried.
>
> "Well," said the prince, "for one kopek (a Russian penny) you can buy a pinch of salt." The children agreed. The prince went into the kitchen and asked the cook to give each of his children a kopek's worth of salt. The children mixed the salt into their soup and the difference was incredible. Now it tasted delicious. And so they learned the value of a penny.

I have never forgotten my mother's story. Even today, if I see a penny on the ground I pick it up! I'm sure a lot of people would think it's silly. But I was brought up to believe that a penny saved is a penny earned. If you save your pennies you will save your dollars as well. That's what I've taught my children and grandchildren.

Cream of Broccoli Soup

Many children as well as adults don't care for broccoli. That's why I came up with the recipe for this soup. It is low in fat and sodium, yet it is so tasty and warming, a perfect light meal on a cold fall day. And, with only three ingredients, you can whip up a batch on a moment's notice.

Makes 5 to 6 servings

1 large head of broccoli, about 2 pounds

1 cup water

1 (12-ounce) can evaporated fat-free milk

¼ teaspoon salt-free garlic-and-herb seasoning

Rinse the broccoli and separate the florets, cutting any large ones in half. Peel the stems and cut any large ones in half.

Place the broccoli florets and stems in a saucepan. Add the water, bring to a boil, and cook until fork-tender, 10 to 15 minutes. Ladle half of the broccoli and half of the cooking liquid into a blender and blend until smooth. Pour the mixture into a large bowl, and repeat with the remaining broccoli and cooking liquid.

Pour all of the puréed broccoli mixture back into the saucepan and add the evaporated milk and the salt-free seasoning. Bring the mixture to a boil over medium heat, stirring constantly. Ladle into bowls and serve hot with croutons.

yiddish word of the day ✡ **shnel** = fast, quick

Cold Spinach Soup

This is an ideal hot-weather soup. The lemon juice in this soup really brightens the flavors, and the eggs make it thick and creamy without adding a lot of fat. I like to serve it in the summertime with diced cucumber and a dollop of sour cream.

 or

Makes 5 to 6 servings

1 pound fresh spinach

6 cups water

½ teaspoon kosher salt

3 to 4 tablespoons lemon juice

2 large eggs

Pepper (optional)

Wash and dry the spinach. Place it in a food processor and process until the spinach is finely chopped.

Place the spinach in a large pot and add the water and the salt. Bring the pot to a boil. Skim off any foam from the top with a large spoon. Turn the heat down to low and simmer for 15 minutes. Add 3 tablespoons of the lemon juice and simmer, uncovered, for 5 minutes more.

Beat the eggs in a large bowl with a whisk. Ladle 3 cups (one at a time!) of the hot spinach mixture into the eggs, whisking constantly so that the soup won't curdle. Pour the remaining spinach mixture into the bowl and whisk to blend. Taste the soup and add more lemon juice, salt, or pepper if needed.

Cool the soup to room temperature, then cover and chill it in the refrigerator until it is cold.

yiddish word of the day ✡ **mentsh = an honorable and decent person**

Yellow Pea Soup with Slices of Frankfurters

I made my version of pea soup many years ago when my children were youngsters and wouldn't eat their vegetables. I added slices of frankfurters and voilà, this did the trick. I could cook various vegetables in my pea soup and purée everything into a smooth, slightly thick soup. Almost every mouthful of soup had a slice of frankfurter. This was appealing to the children and created a competition to see who got the most slices of frankfurters in their bowl of soup.

Makes 6 to 8 servings

7 cups water

1 cup yellow split peas, rinsed

2 low-sodium beef bouillon cubes

1 peeled carrot, cut into thirds

1 peeled parsnip, cut into thirds

1 medium onion, chopped

1 small potato, cubed

3 sprigs fresh parsley

1 bay leaf

2 celery stalks with leaves, cut into thirds

1 garlic clove, chopped (optional)

Kosher salt and pepper to taste (optional)

3 frankfurters, cut into ½-inch slices

In large stockpot, bring the water to a boil. Add the yellow peas, stir, and bring back to boil. Reduce the heat and simmer for 1 hour. Stir often so that peas will not burn. Add bouillon cubes after 1 hour. Simmer for 30 minutes more and then add the carrot, parsnip, onions, potato, parsley, bay leaf, celery, and garlic, if using. Season with salt and pepper if desired. Stir and bring back to a boil over high heat and then reduce the heat to medium and simmer for 30 more minutes, or until the vegetables are tender. Remove the bay leaf and purée the soup in a blender. Do this in batches and be careful not to put too much in the blender at one time. Pour each batch of puréed soup into a large bowl until finished; then pour it all back into the pot. Add the sliced frankfurters and stir over medium low until heated through. If too thick add a little boiled water or broth.

Note: Freeze soup in meal-size portions in separate containers.

yiddish word of the day ✡ **shpeter** = later

The Best Hot Dog I Ever Ate

The saying "good things come to those who wait" makes most people think of the ketchup commercial, but it makes me think of hot dogs. One summer when I was about thirteen years old, I went to stay with my aunt and uncle for a vacation. They lived right near the beach. Every night we went for a walk along the boardwalk.

The boardwalk had all kinds of amusements, like a Ferris wheel, a carousel, and a ring toss. There was also so much delicious food! Roasted nuts, ice cream, pepper steak, and hot dogs as far as the eye could see. The aromas from the food, the colorful lights, and the sounds of carnival music mixed with the crashing waves were magical.

Since I have always kept kosher, I had to be careful about what I ate. Usually, I got a little cup of ice cream that was prepackaged with a kosher insignia. There was only one vendor who sold kosher hot dogs, and he was all the way on the other side of the boardwalk, a couple of miles away.

I enjoyed my ice cream each night (who wouldn't?), but the salty, meaty aroma of hot dogs got more and more enticing with each passing day. Finally one night I said to my cousins, "I am going to get a hot dog tonight!" They looked at me like I was crazy. "Why would you walk all that way for a hot dog when you can have ice cream right here?" they said. "Because I want one," I replied, and set out on my way.

I was determined and I walked and walked and walked. I passed all the familiar vendors and amusements, and then many I had never seen before. My feet got tired and I pulled my thin summer sweater close around me. Just when I thought I might never make it, I reached the kosher hot dog stand.

I plunked my money down on the counter and asked for the biggest hot dog they had. After walking all that distance, I could have eaten six of them! It was juicy and salty and covered in mustard and relish. I ate every last bite and, boy, when I look back I'm proud of the journey I took that night. No hot dog I've ever eaten has tasted as good as that one.

Vegetarian Stew

My daughter came home for her first vacation from college and declared that she was a vegetarian. Oy vey! What was I going to do? But then I started thinking it wasn't so bad. In the Jewish shtetls, meat was very limited. Often, it was reserved for special occasions like holidays or the Sabbath. So I decided to try replacing the meat in some of my family's favorite dishes with tofu. This recipe is one of our favorites.

Makes 5 to 6 servings

1 (12-ounce) package firm or extra-firm tofu

¼ cup all-purpose flour

⅛ teaspoon paprika

¼ teaspoon onion powder

¼ teaspoon garlic powder

Kosher salt and pepper (optional)

1 tablespoon vegetable oil

2 cups peeled, ½-inch diced potatoes (about 3 potatoes)

2 cups peeled, ½-inch diced carrots (about 2 large carrots)

1 parsnip, peeled and cut into ½-inch dice

2 cups peeled, diced turnip (about ½ turnip)

2 medium onions, quartered

Drain the tofu and rinse it with cold water. Pat it dry with paper towels and cut it lengthwise into four equal pieces, then cut each piece crosswise into four equal pieces, making about 1 ½-inch pieces.

In a small bowl stir together the flour, paprika, onion powder, garlic powder, and a pinch of salt and pepper, if using. Roll the tofu pieces in the flour mixture to coat them evenly.

Heat the vegetable oil in a large pot over medium-high heat. Add the tofu pieces and cook for about 1 minute, turning them carefully with a spoon, just until they are lightly crisped on all sides. Transfer the tofu pieces to a plate and set aside.

Add the potatoes, carrots, parsnip, turnip, onions, and garlic to the pot, along with the water. Place the tofu back in the pot, arranging it on top of the vegetables, and bring the mixture to a boil. Lower the heat to a simmer, add the soup mix powder, bay leaf, and allspice berries and stir gently to blend all the ingredients. Cover the pot and simmer for 1 hour 15 minutes, stirring every now and then. The stew is done when the vegetables are fork-tender.

yiddish word of the day ✡ **Oy gevald = Oh my goodness!**

To serve the stew, remove the bay leaf and allspice berries. Ladle the stew onto plates and top each serving with a little bit of chopped fresh dill.

1 large garlic clove, thinly sliced

2 cups water

2 teaspoons pareve imitation beef soup mix powder, or 3 teaspoons vegetable soup mix powder

1 bay leaf

3 whole allspice berries

Chopped fresh dill, for serving

Tomato Soup with Tiny Meatballs

Everyone loves tomato soup and everyone loves meatballs, especially little tiny ones! This recipe combines the two in one. Sugar may seem like an odd ingredient, but it gives the soup a really delicious sweet-and-sour flavor. To make this soup more filling, stir in ½ cup of cooked rice at the end.

Makes 5 to 6 servings

1 pound ground beef

1 cup soft breadcrumbs

1 large egg, lightly beaten

2 tablespoons chopped onions

1 garlic clove, minced

Pinch of pepper

Pinch of nutmeg

6 cups plus 2 tablespoons water, divided

2 (8-ounce) cans tomato sauce

¼ to ⅓ cup granulated sugar

2 tablespoons water

In a large bowl, combine the ground beef, breadcrumbs, egg, onions, garlic, pepper, nutmeg, and 2 tablespoons water. Mix gently with your hands until all the ingredients are combined. Roll the mixture into thirty balls and place them on a plate.

Bring the 6 cups of water to a boil in a large pot, then lower the heat to a simmer. Using a tablespoon, drop each meatball into the water. Be careful so that you don't splash yourself with the boiling water. Gently boil the meatballs for 10 minutes. Stir in the tomato sauce and ¼ cup of sugar. Continue to cook for 30 minutes more. Taste the soup and add a little more sugar if needed. Simmer for another 5 minutes. Let the soup rest for 10 minutes before serving so that the meatballs absorb some of the flavors of the soup.

yiddish word of the day ✡ **Mazltov = Congratulations!**

Meatball Stew

After many attempts at trying to make meatball stew in the way Zadie's mother made it, I have come to the conclusion that certain recipes that a mother prepares for her children cannot be duplicated. Don't compete; after many attempts you will find the one that works for your family. In this case I took the idea of meatball stew and started from scratch, coming up with my own version, and I let Zadie know when I serve it that "this is my special version."

Makes 3 to 6 servings

Meatballs

1 pound ground lean beef

1 cup soft breadcrumbs

1 egg, lightly beaten

¼ cup minced onions

¼ cup water

⅛ teaspoon pepper

1 garlic clove, minced

Stew

1 large onion, roughly chopped

1 tablespoon water

3 medium potatoes, peeled and quartered

1 garlic clove, minced

3 whole allspice berries

Dash of paprika

Pepper (optional)

For the meatballs: In a large bowl mix together the ground beef, breadcrumbs, egg, onions, water, pepper, and garlic and form into six meatballs.

For the stew: In a Dutch oven over medium heat, place the onions and water. Add the meatballs. Cover the pot and cook for 5 minutes until the onions release some liquid. Reduce the heat to low and simmer carefully, stirring often during the next 30 minutes. Check to see that there is some liquid so that it does not burn. Add a little more water, if necessary. Add the potatoes, garlic, allspice, paprika, and pepper, if desired.

Simmer for 30 to 45 minutes more, or until the potatoes are soft. Carefully lift out the meatballs and potatoes. Strain and mash the onions. Pour over the meatballs and potatoes. Serve with cooked green vegetables.

yiddish word of the day ✡ **zadie = grandfather**

Beef Vegetable Soup

When I worked for a company that had its own cafeteria, we always knew what the chef would be serving on Wednesday. It seems that whatever vegetables and beef were left over from lunch on Monday and Tuesday went into a beef and vegetable soup on Wednesday. We always laughed about it. It was so economical I decided to do the same. This soup never comes out the same way twice, but it is always hearty, warming, and filling.

Makes 4 to 6 servings

1 teaspoon olive oil or vegetable oil

½ cup chopped onions

1 stalk celery, sliced crosswise into thin slices

4 cups beef broth (or 2 beef bouillon cubes dissolved in 4 cups water)

1 (14-ounce) can diced tomatoes packed with basil, garlic, and oregano

1 medium potato, peeled and cubed

1 tablespoon orzo (pasta)

1 to 1½ cups cooked leftover vegetables, cut into bite-size pieces

1 cup leftover cooked beef, cut into bite-size pieces

Pepper (optional)

4 cups water

Heat the oil in a pan over medium heat. Sauté the onions and celery first. Pour the broth into a large pot and bring it to a boil. (If you are using bouillon cubes, bring the water to a boil, add the bouillon cubes, and simmer until dissolved.) Add sautéed onions and celery, the tomatoes, potato, orzo, vegetables, and beef to the pot and simmer for 12 to 15 minutes. If the soup looks too thick add a little boiling water. Taste the soup and season with pepper if needed.

Note: You can use a 10-ounce package of mixed frozen vegetables instead of leftover vegetables.

Mushroom Barley Bean Soup

My mother's mushroom barley bean soup was made with meat, bones, and dried mushrooms, which gave the soup a wonderful aroma and taste. However, I wanted to bring this hearty heymish (traditional) and tasty soup up to date. A healthy soup, without the fat and with fresh mushrooms that are easily available, my recipe can be either meat or vegetarian and low sodium. An ideal soup during the winter months. Try it, you'll like it!

 or

Makes 6 to 8 servings

1 tablespoon vegetable oil

1 medium onion, chopped

8 cups water

¼ cup lima beans, rinsed

½ cup pearl barley, rinsed

2 beef or vegetarian low-sodium bouillon cubes

1 cup sliced fresh mushrooms

2 celery stalks, cut into thirds with or without leaves

1 carrot, peeled and diced

1 parsnip, peeled and cut into thirds

1 bay leaf

½ cup peeled and diced yellow turnip (optional)

2 teaspoons chopped fresh dill

Heat the oil in a pan over medium heat. Sauté the onion and set aside. Bring the water to a boil in a large soup pot. Add the beans and barley and bring back to a boil and stir. Reduce the burner to low, cover the pot, and simmer for 1 hour. Stir occasionally so the barley will not stick to the bottom of the pot. Add the bouillon, mushrooms, celery, carrot, parsnip, bay leaf, and turnip, if using. Stir and bring back to a boil over high heat; then reduce the burner back to low and simmer for another hour.

Stir occasionally; taste to check if the barley and bean are soft. Just before serving, stir in the fresh dill and remove the bay leaf.

Note: Soup may become too thick due to the liquid being absorbed by the beans and barley. If so, add a little more boiled hot water. If you prefer to use beef broth, do not use the two beef bouillon cubes and use 4 cups less of water. Replace with 4 cups beef broth.

yiddish word of the day ✡ **bubbe = grandmother**

Eggless Egg Salad

I've read that eating a lot of eggs isn't good for your cholesterol. I may be in my eighties, but I've got a lot of living left to do! I use tofu in place of the eggs. It's so filling and satisfying, I promise you won't even notice the difference. You can serve this as a salad on a bed of lettuce with sliced tomatoes and cucumbers.

Makes 4 to 6 servings

1 (12-ounce) package firm tofu

3 ounces sliced black olives (half of a 6-ounce can)

3 stalks celery, sliced crosswise on the diagonal

1 green bell pepper, diced (or ½ a green pepper and ½ a red pepper)

2 or 3 whole scallions, sliced crosswise on the diagonal

2 tomatoes, diced

½ onion, minced

¼ to ½ cup mayonnaise

1 tablespoon yellow mustard

Kosher salt

Romaine lettuce

Chopped fresh dill or parsley

Paprika

Crumble the tofu in a large bowl. Add the olives, celery, bell pepper, scallions, tomatoes, and onion. In a small bowl, stir together the mayonnaise and mustard. Add the mayonnaise mixture to the tofu mixture and stir until it is evenly mixed. Do this gently so you don't mash up the tofu too much. Season to taste with salt.

To serve buffet style, place 1 or 2 large romaine leaves in a bowl and the eggless egg salad mixture on top, and sprinkle it with the dill and paprika.

yiddish word of the day ✡ **kopveytik = headache**

Meat Cabbage Borsht

The secret ingredient in my cabbage borscht? A beet that I add for color and then take out before serving. It gives the soup such a pretty, ruby-red hue.

Makes 6 to 8 servings

1 (½ to 2 pounds) flanken

9 cups water

1 small cabbage (about 1½ pounds), coarsely shredded (about 4 to 5 cups)

1 medium onion, peeled and diced

2 medium potatoes, peeled and quartered

1 medium carrot, peeled and grated

1 medium beet, peeled and quartered

1 beef bouillon cube

2 cloves garlic, minced

¼ cup freshly squeezed lemon juice, or more to taste

¼ cup granulated sugar, or more to taste

Kosher salt and pepper to taste

Place the flanken in a large stockpot. Add water and bring the pot to a boil. Turn the heat down and skim any foam from the surface with a large spoon. Simmer the flanken for 1 hour.

Add the cabbage, onions, potatoes, carrot, beet, bouillon, and garlic to the pot and stir well. Bring the mixture to a boil, then lower the heat and simmer for 1 hour. Stir in the lemon juice and sugar. Simmer for another 15 minutes.

When the soup is done, remove the beet quarters and discard. Take the flanken out and cut it into bite-size pieces, then add it back to the soup. Taste the soup and season with salt and pepper, or a little more lemon juice or sugar as needed.

Note: "Flanken" is another term for a slab of beef short ribs. Make sure your butcher gives you a good piece! Years ago, the butcher I went to would give out soup and marrow bones with each order for free. If he gave me a lot of bones, I knew the meat was going to be tough. If there were no bones, I knew the meat was going to be perfectly tender.

Bubbe's Burgers

These are the very same hamburgers that my mother used to make for me when I was a little girl. Adding a cup of breadcrumbs to the mix gives hearty flavor and cuts down on the total amount of meat. These burgers are seasoned with garlic, which can be a chore to mince. Here is a tip: place peeled garlic clove on a piece of plastic wrap, add a pinch of salt, wrap the garlic up in the plastic, then give it a few good whacks with the side of a can. Voila! Chopped garlic!

Makes 4 servings

1 pound lean ground beef

1 cup soft breadcrumbs

1 large egg, lightly beaten

2 tablespoons chopped onions

1 garlic clove, minced

Kosher salt and pepper (optional)

2 tablespoons of water

Bulkie rolls, ketchup, mustard, vegetarian baked beans, and kosher pickles, for serving

Heat a large frying pan over medium-high heat. If it's warm outside, you can also heat up your grill. In a large bowl, combine the beef with the breadcrumbs, egg, onions, garlic, salt and pepper to taste (if desired), and the water. Mix the ingredients together with clean hands. Be careful not to overwork it or your burgers will be tough.

Divide the mixture into four parts and pat each into a patty about ½ inch thick. Fry or grill the patties for 8 minutes per side until they are well-done. Place each patty onto a roll and top with your favorite condiments.

yiddish word of the day ✡ **kotletan = hamburger**

Summer

When I was growing up, everyone in our neighborhood lived in three-decker houses. There were people of every nationality and we all got along beautifully. All of the neighbors and all of the children were very close, almost like a large family. Our home was at the top of a hill. There was no such thing as summer camp in those days, so my sisters and I spent our summer vacations playing in the street (there weren't as many cars in those days, either!). After a breakfast of cold cereal, a bulkie roll with butter, juice, and hot cocoa, we headed outside. The boys played baseball or basketball and the girls sat on the front steps. The older girls taught the younger girls how to crochet and embroider. We made hats that we never wore, and we crocheted doilies that we gave to our parents. Sometimes we went on a trip to the library and came home with armfuls of books to read. Among the books that were my favorite was the "Twin Series" by Lucy Fitch Perkins. The books contained an adventure in a different country. Each book would start out by introducing a new set of twins located in different locations and cultural backgrounds. It was both entertaining and educational.

Sometimes, on days that were especially hot and humid, we went to the lake. My mother got up very early in the morning and prepared hamburgers. She would wrap the hamburgers in aluminum foil and then packed them up in a basket with a bag of bulkie rolls, ketchup, mustard, and Half-Sour Pickles (page 52). Then we took the trolley to the lake, which was about twenty minutes away.

We spent the whole day relaxing in the sun, playing by the shore, and swimming in the water. At lunchtime, my mother spread out a big blanket and set up a delicious picnic. What a feast! We were the envy of so many other people. Everyone could smell my mother's delicious hamburgers, the garlic, and the half-sour pickles. Swimming made me very hungry, and though I wasn't normally a big eater, I felt like I could eat two or three hamburgers.

Tomato, Lettuce, and Onion Sandwich

This humble sandwich may not sound like much, but it has special meaning in my family. We eat them whenever anyone is feeling low or depressed. They are instant pick-me-ups! I've left the ingredient list a little bit vague on purpose. Use whatever kinds of bread, lettuce, and cheese you prefer. I like it best on toasted bread with American cheese. This sandwich is especially comforting with potato chips and either hot chocolate or cold chocolate milk.

 or

Makes 1 sandwich

2 slices of bread, toasted

Mayonnaise

Sliced tomatoes

Lettuce leaves

Sliced onions

Sliced cucumbers

Cheese (optional)

Spread a thin layer of mayonnaise on each slice of toasted bread. Layer the tomatoes, lettuce, onions, cucumbers, and cheese (if you are using it) on top of one slice of toast. Cover with the second slice of toast and cut in half diagonally.

yiddish word of the day ✡ **tsibele = onion**

The Bubbe Special
(Tomato, Lettuce, and Onion Sandwich)

When I was a girl, I used to go with my mother to the fruit market. It was very early in the morning. The farmers would bring in fruits and vegetables from their farms on trucks. Before the shopkeepers had time to get the produce inside and put it on display, the customers descended. We bought cucumbers and tomatoes right off the sidewalk. The tomatoes were so incredibly fresh and tasty. I wish the tomatoes at the supermarket today tasted that good. I can still remember their sweet, sun-ripened flavor. And the cucumbers were so delicious. Not like the watery, waxy ones you so often see today. These were small and curvy. They tasted so fresh and clean and were very crunchy.

After we finished shopping, my mother and I would go home. I was always anxious to rush back to join the other children outside. I had games to play and games to watch! We did not want to come into the house to eat at lunchtime so my mother would bring out sandwiches with glasses of chocolate milk, and we would all eat together sitting on the front steps. What would happen if we missed a homerun while watching the boys play baseball!

My children also didn't want to miss out on playtime during the summer so I set up a bench in the backyard where we could sit and eat lunch together along with their friends. Like my mother did for me, the easiest thing for me to make were the same sandwiches with glasses of chocolate milk. They are just the thing after a tiring and busy day when you don't want to eat anything heavy. The taste of the crunchy toast, crisp lettuce, and juicy tomato are so comforting and familiar. It never fails to relax me.

Even today my sisters and I still make lettuce, tomato, and onion sandwiches. Even my grandchildren and son-in-law love them. "What do you want to eat?" is always the first thing I ask them when they come over to the house. "Make me a Bubbe Special!" they often reply—and I am happy to oblige.

Fish

In our family we enjoy fish in various forms: baked, broiled, smoked, and canned. Not only served for lunch and dinner but breakfast as well. There is a tradition to eat fish during the first course at the start of the Friday evening Sabbath meal. Fish is considered pareve (neither meat nor milk) and is great to have recipes for, due to the fact that you can serve it anytime before a meat or dairy meal. Starting with breakfast a variety of fish may be served, such as lox, smoked whitefish, baked herring, fried herring, or pickled salmon in sour cream sauce. For some meals I use canned fish, like tuna and salmon, in my cooking. Extra canned fish is ideal to have on the pantry shelf. It is always available for you. In this chapter I'm going to teach you how to make two of my favorite recipes using canned fish: Tuna Fish Loaf and Salmon Patties. Both are absolutely perfect weeknight meals, and I am sure they will remind you of the dinners your own grandmother used to make.

No chapter about Jewish fish dishes would be complete without a recipe for gefilte fish. Gefilte fish literally means "filled fish." They are oval-shaped balls usually made from a mixture of carp, pike, and whitefish. Traditionally, gefilte fish is eaten on Shabbos and the High Holidays, but I think it's so delicious that I serve it all year round. It makes a great first course! Even if you think you don't like gefilte fish, I suggest you give my version a try. It tastes nothing like the kind that comes from a jar! Bubbe's Gefilte Fish is fluffy and light and not too "fishy." I like to serve it with a lettuce leaf, slice of tomato, and one or two cooked sliced carrots on top. Delicious.

Here are some tips for cooking fish: first, make sure there are no bones! Run your fingers gently over the fish and if you feel any hard bones (they will feel like pins) pull them out with clean tweezers. There is nothing worse than chomping down on a fish bone in the middle of dinner. Second, watch your fish carefully when baking or broiling. Fish can overcook very fast. To find out if the fish is fully cooked, test it with a fork. It should flake easily. Fish is worth your time to keep an eye on and is delicious—for example, Baked Honey Mustard Salmon. Let's get to work and make these fish recipes together. Don't worry if you don't get it right the first time. After a few trial runs you, too, will realize that making fish is easy, and it's healthy!

Easy Baked Fish

Trust me—this recipe is a winner. Many years ago I was listening to the radio when an advertisement for mayonnaise came on. The company was sponsoring a recipe contest. Send in a recipe that used their mayonnaise, and you could win two front row tickets to see Frank Sinatra! I entered this fish recipe, and I won! I couldn't believe it. I was the envy of all my friends. Every time I prepare this dish, I remember what a magical evening the night of the concert was.

 or

Makes 4 servings

1 (1-pound) cod fillet, or haddock, or any other white kosher fish, cut into 4 pieces

¼ cup breadcrumbs

¼ teaspoon paprika

½ teaspoon chopped fresh dill (optional)

½ teaspoon freshly grated lemon zest

Kosher salt and pepper

1 tablespoon vegetable oil

1 tablespoon mayonnaise

Preheat the oven to 450°F. Line a small baking sheet with foil and spray it with nonstick cooking spray.

Combine the breadcrumbs, paprika, dill, lemon zest, and a pinch of salt and pepper on a plate. Add the vegetable oil and mix with a spoon until all the breadcrumbs are moistened.

Spread the mayonnaise evenly over both sides of the fish. Dredge the fish in the breadcrumb mixture. Make sure to coat it on both sides.

Place the fish on the baking sheet and bake the fish until it flakes easily with a fork, about 12 minutes.

yiddish word of the day ✡ **mitsve = good deed**

Baked Honey Mustard Salmon

One day when my grandson was still in grade school, he went on a field trip with his class. They stopped at a kosher dairy restaurant for lunch. Most of the children ordered pizza or tuna sandwiches, but my grandson recognized the salmon on the menu as a dish his Bubbe often made. The other kids teased him for ordering such a grown-up meal, but when the food arrived they all wanted a taste. There was none left over for my grandson! I like to think I played a role in introducing his whole class to healthy, delicious fish.

The honey-mustard glaze in this recipe might cause your salmon to brown slightly around the edges as it cooks. Watch it carefully to make sure it doesn't burn. Leftovers are great over green salad!

Makes 3 to 4 servings

1 (1-pound) salmon fillet, cut crosswise into 3 or 4 pieces

Vegetable oil or nonstick cooking spray

1½ tablespoons honey

1 tablespoon brown mustard

Preheat the oven to 450°F. Grease a baking sheet with vegetable oil or spray it with nonstick spray. Place the salmon pieces on the baking sheet with the skin side facing down. In a small bowl, stir together the honey and mustard. Spread the honey-mustard mixture over the salmon. Bake the salmon for 10 to 12 minutes, until the fish is just cooked through. To test it, cut into the middle just a little bit with a fork. The fish should be just opaque in the middle.

yiddish word of the day ✡ **lebedik** = lively, alive

Baked Fish Cakes

Fish cakes are part of the recipes that my mother made for me growing up. They were a tradition in my home since we had them about once a week. There are so many kinds, and so many recipe variations! I have been making my version for years, and everyone thinks they are the best: crunchy on the outside and tender on the inside, with a little kick from the sweet red pepper sauce. The creamy mashed potatoes make these cakes extra comforting. Anyone who thinks they don't like fish loves them, and of course they are budget-friendly!

Makes 12 cakes, serving 6

Cakes

3 tablespoons kosher margarine or unsalted butter

1 pound cod or haddock fillets

4 medium potatoes

¼ cup milk

Kosher salt and pepper

1 medium onion, peeled and minced

1 large egg, lightly beaten

1 cup breadcrumbs

Sauce

6 tablespoons mayonnaise

4 tablespoons sweet red pepper relish

First, cook the fish. Heat 2 tablespoons of the margarine in a large frying pan over medium-low heat. Add the fish and cook just until it is cooked through and flakes easily. Place the fish on a plate and shred it with a fork.

Next, cook the potatoes. Peel the potatoes and cut each one into eight pieces. Place the potatoes in a medium saucepan and add just enough water to cover. Bring it to a boil, then turn down the heat to low and cook until the potatoes are tender, about 15 minutes. Drain the potatoes and return them to the pan. Add the remaining tablespoon of margarine and the milk. Mash the potatoes well with a fork or a potato masher. Taste the potatoes and season them with salt and pepper if needed.

Now it's time to make the fish cakes. Combine the fish and the mashed potato mixture in a large bowl. Add the onions and the egg and mix everything together. Place the bowl in the refrigerator and chill for 2 hours.

yiddish word of the day ✡ **balabusta = homemaker**

Preheat the oven to 375°F. Grease a baking sheet or spray it with nonstick spray.

When the fish mixture is chilled take it out of the refrigerator. Take 2 tablespoons of the mixture at a time and form into 2-inch balls. You will get about twelve balls. Then flatten each one into small round cakes. Place the breadcrumbs on a plate. Coat the cakes in the breadcrumbs and place them carefully onto the prepared baking sheet. Bake the cakes for 25 to 30 minutes, until they are well browned.

To make the sauce, combine the mayonnaise with the relish in a small bowl. Stir until well combined. Serve the cakes with the sauce on the side.

Salmon Patties with Lemon Sauce

If you want to get fancy, you can call these salmon croquettes. Pan-fried salmon patties are a classic alternative to a hamburger since they can be served before a dairy meal or be part of a pareve meal, but I prefer to serve them on a plate. There are gourmet versions with special sauces and expensive added ingredients, but I think nothing tastes better than my traditional, original recipe. If you like dill, add a pinch to both the cakes and the sauce. They can be prepared quickly and make a great weeknight meal. This is an ideal meal that is not too heavy but filling.

 or

Makes 4 servings

Salmon Patties

1 (16-ounce) can salmon

2 tablespoons pareve margarine or unsalted butter

½ cup chopped onions

1 cup breadcrumbs

2 large eggs, lightly beaten

1 teaspoon chopped fresh dill (optional)

2 tablespoons vegetable oil

Lemon Sauce (optional)

2 tablespoons margarine or butter

2 tablespoons all-purpose flour

⅛ teaspoon kosher salt

Drain the salmon but make sure to save the liquid. Check the fish with a fork and take out any skin and bones. Flake the salmon in a large bowl and set it aside.

Heat the margarine in a nonstick skillet and add the onions. Sauté for a few minutes until the onions are soft and translucent. Place the onions in the bowl with the salmon and add ⅓ cup of the breadcrumbs, the eggs, and the dill (if you are using it). Add ¼ cup of the saved liquid from the salmon can (just enough to moisten the salmon!) and mix everything together well. Add more liquid if the mixture is too dry; add more breadcrumbs if it's too soft.

Form the salmon mixture into four patties that are all the same size. Coat the patties in the remaining breadcrumbs.

Heat the vegetable oil in a large frying pan over medium heat. Add the patties and cook for 3 to 4 minutes per side, until they are nice and browned. Lift them out carefully with a spatula.

yiddish word of the day ✡ **shmeykhl** = smile

To make the Lemon Sauce, melt the margarine in a small pot. Stir in the flour, salt, and pepper. Add the milk slowly and cook over medium heat, stirring often, until the sauce is thick and bubbling. Stir in the lemon juice and cook for 2 more minutes. Remove the sauce from the heat and stir in the dill (if you are using it).

Serve the salmon patties hot, either topped with the Lemon Sauce or with the sauce on the side.

Pinch of pepper

1 cup milk

2 teaspoons lemon juice

1 tablespoon chopped fresh dill (optional)

Gefilte Fish

Not everyone likes gefilte fish, but my recipe tastes nothing like the jarred versions you get at the supermarket. Mine are light and fluffy and not too "fishy." I like to serve gefilte fish with a lettuce leaf, a slice of tomato, and one or two cooked sliced carrots on top and a little bit of horseradish (page 57). To prepare them from scratch, you will need a total of three pounds of fish. It doesn't have to be exactly one pound of each, but it should be a mixture of pike, which is a lean fish, and a fatty fish, like whitefish or carp.

If you're short on time, or fresh fish is not available, use a frozen gefilte fish blend, which is available at many supermarkets and kosher stores. It's ready to cook—just follow the directions on the package. How easy is that?

Makes 6 servings

Fish

1 pound whitefish fillets

1 pound pike fillets

1 pound carp fillets

2 onions, peeled and finely chopped

2 large eggs, lightly beaten

2 to 4 tablespoons matzo meal

1 teaspoon kosher salt

½ teaspoon sugar, or more if you want it sweeter

⅛ teaspoon pepper

2 tablespoons to ¼ cup cold water

First, make the gefilte fish balls. Place the whitefish, pike, and carp in a food processor and pulse until the fish is finely ground. Add the onions and pulse two or three more times to incorporate them. Place the fish mixture in a large bowl and add the eggs, 2 tablespoons of the matzo meal, the salt, sugar, pepper, and enough cold water to moisten the fish. Gently mix the ingredients until they are thoroughly blended. If the mixture seems too wet, add another tablespoon or two of matzo meal. With wet hands use about ¼ cup of the mixture at a time to form into six balls, flattening them slightly so that they are more oval-shaped.

Next, make the poaching liquid. Place the fish heads and bones into a very large stockpot. Add the onions and onion skins, carrots, and salt. Add the water and bring to a boil over medium-high heat. Reduce the heat to low and carefully lower the gefilte fish balls into the pot. (If it's boiling too rapidly, the fish balls will fall apart.)

yiddish word of the day ✡ **tsores= trouble**

Cover the pot and cook the gefilte fish for 1 hour, checking them occasionally and skimming any foam from the surface with a large spoon. Remove the lid from the pot and continue to cook the gefilte fish for an additional 30 minutes. Taste the liquid and add more salt or pepper, or a pinch of sugar, as needed.

Cool the gefilte fish balls slightly, then place them into a large bowl. Pour the poaching liquid through a sieve. Save the carrots but throw out the onions and onion skins and fish head and bones. Cut the carrots into slices and add them to the bowl with the gefilte fish. Chill the gefilte fish in the refrigerator until it is cold. Serve the gefilte fish with horseradish and the carrots on lettuce leaves.

Poaching Liquid

Fish heads and bones (have the fish monger give you these when you buy the fish fillets)

2 onions, peeled and sliced, skins reserved

2 large carrots, peeled and cut crosswise into thirds

1 teaspoon kosher salt

2 quarts water

1/8 teaspoon pepper

Sugar (optional)

Homemade Horseradish (page 57), for serving

Sole Stuffed with Salmon

This is an easy, elegant dish that I like to serve when company comes over for dinner. The white sole and the pink salmon look so pretty wrapped up together on the plate. Pair it with green beans or broccoli and plenty of rice to soak up the creamy, citrusy Lemon Sauce.

 or

Makes 6 servings

6 skinless sole fillets (about 1 pound total)

1 skinless salmon fillet (½ to ¾ pound), cut into 6 equal pieces about 2 inches long and 1½ inches wide

Paprika

Lemon Sauce (optional; page 92)

Preheat the oven to 400°F. Grease a 9 x 9-inch baking pan or spray it with nonstick spray.

Place one piece of sole on a plate with a short end facing you. Place a piece of salmon on top of the sole. Beginning with the end closest to you, roll the fish up carefully. Place the fish, seam side down, in the prepared baking pan. Do the same thing with remaining pieces of sole and salmon.

Sprinkle the fish with paprika and bake for 12 to 15 minutes, until the fish flakes easily with a fork.

Serve the fish topped with the Lemon Sauce.

yiddish word of the day ✡ **sholfn = sleep**

Tuna Fish Loaf

Like a lot of bubbes, I love bargains. And here is a tip: cooking with canned fish is a big one! Not only is tuna fish often on sale, but it lasts for a very long time on the shelf. When you cook with canned fish, you don't have to go to the store at the last minute, and you don't have to use it right away. My tuna fish loaf is a bit like meatloaf, but much healthier. I love the little kick the paprika sprinkled on top gives this dish. Serve it with baked potatoes or French fries and a green vegetable, like spinach or broccoli.

Makes 4 servings

1 tablespoon margarine or butter

2 slices white bread

1 cup milk

2 (5-ounce) cans water-packed tuna, drained

1 medium onion, peeled and grated

1 stalk celery, grated

2 large eggs, lightly beaten

Pinch of kosher salt

Pinch of paprika

Preheat the oven to 350°F. Place the margarine in the bottom of a 9 x 5-inch loaf pan and place the loaf pan in the oven just until the margarine is melted. Set it aside.

Place the bread slices in a medium bowl. Heat the milk in a small saucepan until it is just warm. Pour the milk over the bread.

Flake the tuna in another bowl. Add the onions and celery to the tuna along with the eggs. Add the tuna mixture to the bread mixture and season with salt. Stir everything together well with a large spoon.

Pour the mixture into the prepared loaf pan and sprinkle the top with paprika. Bake for 45 minutes. Cool the loaf a little bit before serving.

yiddish word of the day ✡ **oyern** = ears

Poultry & Meat

I often receive emails from new brides striving to re-create their husband's favorite dishes. "Help!" they say. "How do I make a perfect roast chicken?" or "What is the secret to preparing pot roast just like his mother's?"

Their questions always make me think of when I was a newlywed many years ago. My husband's all-time favorite dish was his mother's meatball stew. In the first months of our marriage I tried many times to prepare it. I lined up all the ingredients on the counter and followed the instructions carefully; simmering the meatballs, tasting the sauce to make sure that it was seasoned just right. But each night when we sat down to dinner Zadie would say, "Honey, they're very good. But not quite as good as my mother's." Oy! Even today, he still claims that his mother's meatballs were better than mine.

I guess in that way history is bound to repeat itself. I remember my father telling my mother that certain recipes she made did not compare to his own mother's. It seems that some foods that a fellow's mother makes cannot be duplicated—even if the recipe and ingredients are exactly the same. My advice to young couples just starting out is: don't try to compete! Focus on making dishes with flavors that you enjoy. Pretty soon you will have many recipes that you both love. And, you will find out that you are a very good cook in your own right.

In this chapter I've included three recipes for meatballs: my famous tangy Sweet and Sour Meatballs, a hearty Chicken and Meatball Fricassee, and my family's favorite Spaghetti and Meatballs. I have not included Zadie's mother's meatball stew! Instead I make my own version, which I included earlier in the book. Over the years I finally gave up trying to make her dish just right and concentrated on preparing new dishes instead. You should, too! I hope you find lots of inspiration in this chapter.

When I was growing up, poultry and beef were expensive and many of the dishes we enjoy today were considered a luxury back then. So, I had to learn to make the most of what was available, such as leftover soup chicken, turkey drumsticks, or inexpensive cuts of beef. I found ways to coax flavor out of them all, whether by seasoning poultry with a whole bunch of herbs, garlic, and onions or cooking beef slowly until it is tender. My recipes for Turkey Egg Rolls, Chicken Rice Casserole, Pepper Steak, and Bubbe's Shepherd's Pie are so delicious, you would never guess they are also budget-friendly.

Of course, sometimes it is worth it to splurge, especially around the holidays. In this chapter I've also shared my family's favorite special-occasion recipes for Stuffed Breast of Veal, Lamb Stew, Bubbe's Brisket, and of course my perfect Roast Chicken, with crispy skin and moist, flavorful meat.

Easy Chicken Schnitzel

The ingredients for my chicken schnitzel are so simple: chicken breasts, breadcrumbs, flour, an egg, and garlic powder and onion powder for seasoning. Today, it's one of my grandchildren's favorite things to have for dinner. It also has roots in Israel, where turkey schnitzel is a common dish.

I like to serve chicken schnitzel with a side of sautéed carrots and steamed string beans. If you make this dish a little ahead of time, you can keep the chicken warm in a 200° to 250°F oven. Or, freeze the chicken wrapped in aluminum foil. Reheat in a 400°F oven for several minutes.

Makes 4 servings

1 large egg

¼ cup water

⅓ cup all-purpose flour

Garlic powder, to taste

Onion powder, to taste

Kosher salt and pepper, to taste

⅔ cup breadcrumbs

4 boneless, skinless chicken breasts

2 to 3 tablespoons vegetable oil

Beat the egg and water together in a bowl. In a separate bowl, mix together the flour, garlic powder, onion powder, salt, and pepper. Pour the flour mixture onto a plate. Spread the breadcrumbs onto a second plate.

Remove any visible fat from the chicken breasts. Place the chicken breasts between two sheets of plastic wrap and hammer them with a mallet or rolling pin until they are about ¼ inch thick. Working with one chicken breast at a time, lightly coat them in the flour mixture on both sides and shake off the excess. Dip them in the egg mixture, and then coat them in the breadcrumbs, coating the chicken breasts on all sides. Pat them lightly so that the breadcrumbs stick to the chicken.

Heat the oil in a large frying pan over medium heat. Add the chicken breasts to the pan and cook for 3 minutes. Turn the chicken and continue to cook for 3 to 4 minutes more, until the coating is golden and crispy and the chicken is cooked through.

Note: Matzo meal is okay for breading, but I prefer to use breadcrumbs.

yiddish word of the day ✡ **ongeblozn = pompous and conceited**

Schmaltz and Gribenes

Schmaltz (rendered chicken fat) is an important ingredient in many Jewish recipes. It is delicious in place of the oil in my Chopped Chicken Liver (page 36) and my Black Radish Salad (page 55), and it adds so much flavor to egg salad and mashed potatoes. However, it isn't very healthy, so these days I usually make a substitute with sautéed onion and ¼ cup vegetable oil. Gribenes, also known as cracklings, are the fried bits of chicken skin that are the byproduct of making schmaltz, and they are a crispy, addictive snack!

Makes ½ cup

Skin and fat from 1 or 2 chickens

1 large onion, peeled and chopped

Cut as much skin and fat from the lower part of the chicken or chickens as you can. Save the chickens for another recipe. Cut the skin and fat into small pieces and put it in a small, heavy pot. Add the onion and cook over medium heat until the fat melts, stirring occasionally so that the onion doesn't burn. Turn the heat down to low and continue to cook for 10 minutes until the onions are golden and the chicken cracklings are brown and crisp. Cool everything a little bit and then strain the fat into a glass jar. Be careful! It is very hot. Place the cracklings in a small container. Store both in the refrigerator.

yiddish word of the day ✡ **feter = uncle**

Roast Chicken

When I was a little girl, I would help my mother do the food shopping for Shabbos, the Sabbath meal. Every week we would visit the butcher, the vegetable market, and the bakery. On the street, in front of the shops, were elderly women—Jewish bubbes—sitting in folding chairs and asking for change. From Wednesday through Friday morning they sat there, and then they pooled their money and used it to buy chicken, fish, and challah for those less fortunate in the neighborhood, so that they could have a good Shabbos, too. In the old days, before there were big charity organizations, that's how *mitzvahs*, or good deeds, were done.

Roast chicken is a very meaningful dish for Jewish families. It is traditionally eaten each week for the Sabbath meal. Kosher chickens are soaked in cold water and salted according to the kosher dietary laws, making them extremely flavorful! I know a lot of people who aren't Jewish but always buy kosher chickens because they taste so much better.

This recipe is how my mother made roast chicken, how I make it, and how I taught my children to make it.

Makes 4 to 5 servings

1 (3 to 4 pound) roasting chicken

Boiling water

Garlic powder

Onion powder

Paprika

Dried rosemary (optional)

3 or 4 whole allspice berries

Preheat the oven to 350°F. Take the giblets out of the chicken and keep them for making chicken soup. Cut away any excess fat or skin. Rinse the chicken under the cold water faucet. Place the chicken in a large bowl and pour boiling water over it. Then rinse with cold water and pluck any pin feathers from the wings and drumsticks with tweezers or a small knife.

Place the chicken breast-side up in a roasting pan and sprinkle it with lots of garlic powder, onion powder, paprika, and dried rosemary (if you are using it). Tuck 1 or 2 of the allspice berries under the skin. Turn the chicken breast-side down and sprinkle with more garlic powder, onion powder, paprika, and dried

---

yiddish word of the day ✡ **tsdoke or tzedakah= to help those less fortunate**

rosemary (if you are using it). Place the remaining one or two allspice berries in the cavity of the chicken.

Place the chicken in the oven and roast for 1 hour 30 minutes, until the skin is crispy and the juices run clear when a knife is inserted into the thickest part of the thigh. Let the chicken rest in the pan for 10 to 15 minutes, then turn it breast-side up and transfer it to a serving platter.

Note: The chicken may not be as browned as in pictures of roast chicken because the chicken is baked with breast-side down in the pan, but the juices go into the breasts and the chicken is not as dry.

Chicken Drumettes

These chicken drumettes are a little bit like kosher Buffalo wings! The sweet and sour sauce, ketchup, and garlic and onion powder make such an addictive and flavorful glaze. This is a great dish to serve as part of a casual buffet. For a lower-fat version, you can remove all the skin from the chicken drumettes before you cook them.

Makes 3 to 4 servings

2 to 3 pounds chicken wings

¼ cup duck sauce or sweet and sour sauce

1½ teaspoons ketchup

¾ teaspoon garlic powder

¾ teaspoon onion powder

¼ teaspoon vinegar

¼ teaspoon soy sauce

Cut away any excess fat from the chicken wings. Place them in a large bowl and pour boiling water over them. Then rinse with cold water and pluck any pin feathers from the wings with tweezers. Using a sharp knife, cut the wings in half at the joint. (Reserve the bony part of the wing for chicken soup!) Place the drumettes in a large zip-top plastic bag.

In a medium bowl, whisk together the duck sauce, ketchup, garlic powder, onion powder, vinegar, and soy sauce. Then, pour it over the chicken. Seal the bag shut and refrigerate overnight.

Preheat the oven to 400°F. Transfer the chicken wings to a baking dish lined with aluminum foil. Bake the chicken for 15 to 20 minutes, until it is cooked through.

yiddish word of the day ✡ **fartik = finished or done**

Crispy Baked Chicken

This chicken makes a great lunch for the beach or a picnic. Bake it early in the morning. Let it cool, and then wrap it in aluminum foil. Serve it with Half-Sour Pickles (page 52) and vegetarian baked beans. Don't forget the lemonade!

Makes 4 servings

4 to 6 chicken pieces

1 cup cornflake crumbs

1 teaspoon onion powder

1½ teaspoons garlic powder

Vegetable oil cooking spray

Heat the oven to 400°F. Cut away any excess fat from the chicken pieces. Place the chicken in a large bowl and pour boiling water over it. Then rinse with cold water and pluck out any pin feathers with tweezers.

Mix the cornflake crumbs, onion powder, and garlic powder in a bowl. Spray the chicken pieces with the vegetable oil cooking spray and roll them in the cornflake mixture. Place the chicken in a baking pan and bake for 40 to 45 minutes. To see if the chicken is done, cut into the middle of one piece. If you see any pink, cook it for a few minutes more.

yiddish word of the day ✡ **farblondzshet** = **lost**

Chicken Rice Casserole

This recipe only has four ingredients, but the onion soup mix adds a lot of flavor. It's great if you are just learning how to cook. If you're going to have a busy day, you can prepare everything in the morning and put the casserole in the refrigerator. Then just pop it in the oven as soon as you get home. By the time you are ready to sit down and eat, the chicken is done!

Makes 4 servings

1 fryer chicken (about 3½ to 4 pounds) cut into 4 pieces

1 cup rice

1 package onion soup mix

1 teaspoon pareve margarine

Rinse the chicken pieces. Place them in a large bowl and pour boiling water over them. Then rinse with cold water and pluck any pin feathers from the wings and drumsticks with tweezers.

Heat the oven to 400°F. Grease a 10 x 7-inch casserole dish.

Cook the rice according to the instructions on the back of the box. Spoon the rice into the casserole dish and dot it with the margarine.

Spread the onion soup mix on a plate. Roll the chicken pieces in the soup mix and place them on top of the rice, skin-side up. Sprinkle any onion soup mix that didn't stick to the chicken over the top. Cover the casserole with aluminum foil and bake for 50 to 60 minutes.

yiddish word of the day ✡ **fiss = legs**

Mock Gefilte Fish

This is a very old recipe in my family. I don't make it too often, but it's really good if you want to serve traditional Jewish gefilte fish to someone who doesn't like fish—it's made with chicken instead! Mock gefilte fish is a little more mild in flavor. Garnish each serving with the cooked carrots and some horseradish sauce.

Makes 6 servings

1 pound ground chicken

1 large egg

1 medium onion, peeled and grated

½ cup matzo meal

1½ teaspoons kosher salt, divided

Pinch of pepper

2 tablespoons water

2 large carrots, peeled and sliced diagonally

1 large onion, peeled and quartered (save the onion skin)

1 stalk celery, cut into three pieces

2 teaspoons sugar

6 cups water

In a large bowl, combine the ground chicken, egg, grated onion, matzo meal, ¾ teaspoon of the salt, pepper, and the water. Mix the ingredients together with clean hands until they are well blended. With wet hands shape the mixture into six balls, making them slightly oval shape.

Rinse the onion skins under cold water and place them with the carrots, quartered onion, celery, sugar, and remaining salt in a large stockpot. Add the water and bring to a boil over medium-high heat.

Carefully drop the chicken balls one by one into the pot and simmer them over low heat for 20 to 30 minutes, until the chicken is cooked through and the vegetables are fork-tender.

Cool the chicken balls in the cooking liquid. Then, place the balls in a bowl. Strain the liquid through a sieve over the chicken balls. Save the carrots, but throw away the rest of the vegetables. Serve the carrots with the mock gefilte fish balls.

Note: Onion skins will help add a little color to the mock gefilte fish and add to the overall appearance.

Tasty Soup Chicken

After you make chicken stock, what should you do with the leftover cooked chicken? A good bubbe never lets food go to waste. At first I tried serving it plain, but boiled chicken is dry and tasteless. My children didn't care for it one bit. So I came up with this recipe, which seasons the chicken with onion powder, garlic powder, and paprika. It's so quick and simple, and you probably already have everything you need in the cabinet (except for the chicken, of course!).

Sometimes I serve this dish with the soup I originally used the chicken to make. Other times, I serve it with cranberry sauce or pickles and a green vegetable. It also makes delicious chicken salad.

Makes 4 servings

Leftover boiled chicken from Chicken Soup with Matzo Balls (page 60)

Vegetable oil cooking spray

Onion powder

Garlic powder

Paprika

Preheat the broiler. Line a baking pan with aluminum foil and place the chicken in it. Spray the chicken lightly on all sides with the vegetable oil spray. Then, sprinkle it lightly with the onion powder, garlic powder, and paprika on all sides. Broil the chicken for 1 to 2 minutes on each side, just until it starts to brown.

yiddish word of the day ✡ **shvebele = matchstick**

Turkey Egg Rolls

When it comes to Chinese food, I love egg rolls best. This is a delicious recipe to make any time of the year, but especially after Thanksgiving, when you have all that leftover turkey. I like to serve these with a little duck sauce mixed with two tablespoons of water and heated until warm, or serve them with cranberry sauce: mash the cranberry sauce with a fork and then heat the sauce with a little water. It tastes delicious and is something different for the family to enjoy.

Makes 6 to 8 servings

1 tablespoon vegetable oil

¾ cup chopped onions

½ cup chopped celery (about 1 rib)

½ cup peeled and shredded carrot (about 1 small carrot)

2½ cups chopped cooked turkey or chicken

2 large eggs, lightly beaten

¼ teaspoon garlic powder

Kosher salt and pepper

1 package egg roll wrappers

1 tablespoon vegetable oil

Heat the vegetable oil in a large frying pan over medium heat. Add the onion, celery, and carrot and cook until the vegetables are beginning to turn soft, about 2 to 3 minutes. Add the turkey or chicken and cook for 1 minute.

Scrape the turkey mixture out of the frying pan and into a large bowl. Stir in the eggs and garlic powder, and season to taste with salt and pepper. Let the mixture cool to room temperature.

Now the egg rolls. Place one egg roll wrapper on a work surface with one corner facing you. Place 2 tablespoons of the turkey mixture in the middle of the wrapper. Beginning with the corner closest to you, roll the wrapper over the filling and fold in the sides. Dip your finger in a little water and press it along the seams to help the roll stay closed. Repeat with remaining wrappers and filling.

Heat the vegetable oil in a large frying pan over medium heat. Working in batches if you need to, add the rolls, seam side down, to the pan. Fry for 2 or 3 minutes a side, until the rolls are golden brown and crispy. Transfer the rolls to a paper towel–lined plate to drain. Serve warm.

yiddish word of the day ✡ **takeh = Oh really? or Is that so?**

Five Turkeys!

A new supermarket opened up in the neighborhood right before Thanksgiving. I went shopping one morning and noticed a big sign in the meat department advertising frozen kosher turkeys at 89¢ a pound. I found the manager and asked him if he made a mistake. Frozen turkeys cost $1.99 a pound in all the other markets!

"Well," said the manager, "these turkeys are an unadvertised in-store promotion."

"How much of a sale?" I asked. I still couldn't believe my eyes. I needed to hear the manager say the price out loud.

"Eighty-nine cents a pound," he said.

"Really? Are you sure?"

"Lady, I am the manager. Of course I'm sure. We have two or three hundred turkeys, and I'd like to sell them all before Thanksgiving. Call your friends and tell them."

"Is there any limit on how many we can buy?"

Time to make the turkey

"No, no limits. First come, first served."

Well, what do you think happened? I went home and called everyone I could think of! I called my daughters. I called my sisters. I called everybody with large families. "Go down as fast as you can. Kosher turkeys! Not $1.99 a pound, only 89¢!" At first they didn't believe me. "Trust me," I said. "I talked to the manager. There's not even a limit."

Everyone hurried to the store and cleaned out all the turkeys. I went down myself later that afternoon. Most of the turkeys were gone, but way down at the bottom I saw a few left. I leaned over, reached down, and hauled a massive twelve- or fourteen-pound turkey into my shopping cart.

I admit I started to get a little greedy. One, that I would cook right away. Two, it would be good to have one in the freezer. Three, well you never know. Four, I have room. Five, I could cut it up and cook it in various ways. Each time I had to reach down a bit further into the freezer to lug out a turkey. I looked around the store to make sure I didn't know any of the other shoppers. I was beginning to feel embarrassed!

When I got home, I put four of the turkeys in the freezer and one in the refrigerator to thaw. But the next day, I couldn't get out of bed. My back hurt so much from picking up the turkeys! My back hurt for over a month. Finally, I went to the doctor and told him what happened. "What are you going to do with five turkeys," he said. "Feed an army?"

Later, I went back to the supermarket and the manager thanked me. He said, "You certainly let all your friends know! We sold out of turkeys in a day and a half. Thank you!" Since then I have helped out the manager in many ways. I tell him about the Jewish holidays, and what he should stock up on for them. Now, he carries all sorts of things for Passover, like matzo, coconut macaroons, and other delicacies. But nothing will ever top those turkeys!

Sweet and Sour Turkey Drumsticks

Most people have turkey for a holiday meal just once a year, on Thanksgiving. But many Jewish people also have a turkey dinner for Purim, the festival that celebrates Jewish survival with parades, costumes, and the giving of charity. The oppressive King Ahasuerus ruled from India to Ethiopia. In Hebrew, the word *hodu* means both turkey (tarnegol hodu) and India. Poppy seeds (mohn) are also traditional for Purim, so I like to serve these drumsticks with egg noodles tossed with olive oil sprinkled with poppy seeds.

Makes 4 servings

1 cup sweet and sour sauce or duck sauce

2 tablespoons ketchup

2 teaspoons garlic powder

1 teaspoon onion powder

2 teaspoons soy sauce

1 teaspoon vinegar

1 teaspoon spicy brown mustard (optional)

4 turkey drumsticks

Boiling water

Mix together the sweet and sour sauce, ketchup, garlic powder, onion powder, soy sauce, vinegar, and mustard (if you're using it) in a medium bowl.

Place the turkey drumsticks in a large bowl. Pour the boiling water over them. Then rinse the drumsticks with cold water and check for any pin feathers. If you see any, pluck them out with tweezers.

Place the drumsticks on a plate and spoon enough of the sauce over them to coat them. Place the drumsticks in a slow cooker or crock pot and pour the rest of the sauce over them. Cover the pot and cook on high for 30 minutes, then reduce heat to low and cook for 6 to 7 hours.

Serve one whole drumstick per person. Or you can also cut the meat off the bone and serve it that way. Just be sure to spoon plenty of the delicious sauce over them!

yiddish word of the day ✡ **veter = weather**

Turkey Cacciatore

Several years ago I made enough turkey cacciatore to serve ten people. I froze it all, and then I packed it in my suitcase and took it on a plane to California. I was going to visit my son, who loves my turkey cacciatore! It was still frozen when I arrived at his home? I'm sure the security people didn't know what to make of all the food in my suitcase, I was on a mission to feed my family a delicious home-cooked meal.

Makes 4 servings

1 large egg

¼ cup water

2 tablespoons all-purpose flour

2 tablespoons matzo meal

1 pound boneless, skinless turkey breast cutlets

2 tablespoons extra-virgin olive oil

1 large onion, peeled, sliced and separated into rings

1 large garlic clove, peeled and minced (about 1 teaspoon)

1 (6-ounce) can tomato paste

¼ teaspoon Italian seasoning (or a pinch each of pepper, oregano, basil, and thyme)

1 cup boiling water

½ cup sliced fresh button mushrooms or a can of stems and pieces

Beat the egg and the water together in a large bowl. Spread the flour on a plate and the matzo meal on another plate. Remove any visible fat from the turkey cutlets. Place the turkey breast cutlets between two pieces of plastic wrap and pound with a meat mallet until they are ½ inch thick. Coat each cutlet in the flour on both sides and shake off the excess. Dip it into the egg mixture, then coat it in the matzo meal. Place the cutlets aside on a plate.

Heat 1 tablespoon of the olive oil in a large skillet (with a lid) over medium heat. Add the onions and garlic and cook for 2 minutes and then push to the edge of the pan. Add the remaining tablespoon of olive oil and let it heat up for a few seconds. Add the turkey cutlets and cook until lightly browned on each side, about 2 minutes.

Mix together the tomato paste, Italian seasoning, and boiling water in a bowl. Pour the tomato mixture over the cutlets. Cover the skillet and turn the heat down to low. Simmer until the turkey is tender and cooked through, about 35 minutes. Add the mushrooms and continue to cook for 5 minutes.

Transfer the turkey cutlets to a plate and serve topped with the sauce. Serve with pasta or rice.

yiddish word of the day ✡ **bissel = little bit**

Bubbe's Brisket

"Bubbe make brisket! Bubbe make brisket! Bubbe make brisket!" wrote one of the biggest fans of *Feed Me Bubbe*. How could I refuse? Here are my two favorite recipes for this classic, comforting dish. The first, which is my family's favorite, includes honey and chile sauce. The second is made with a secret ingredient your dinner guests will never guess—onion soup mix! I like to serve brisket with mashed potatoes and steamed green beans, but you also can't go wrong with Kasha Varnishkes (page 154).

Makes 5 or 6 servings

1 brisket (3 to 4 pounds), preferably first cut

2 medium onions, sliced

½ cup chile sauce

⅓ cup honey

½ teaspoon garlic powder

½ to ¾ cup water

Kosher salt and pepper, to taste

Heat the oven to 325°F. Place the brisket in a medium-size roasting pan with a lid and scatter the onions on top. In a small bowl, combine the chile sauce, honey, garlic powder, and ½ cup water. Season the mixture with a pinch of salt and pepper. Pour the mixture over the brisket.

Put the lid on the roasting pan or cover tightly with two layers of aluminum foil. Place it in the oven, and bake for 1½ hours. Take the brisket out of the oven and lift cover gently to see if there is enough liquid in the pan. If it looks dry, add a little more water. Place the brisket back in the oven and continue to cook for another 1½ to 2 hours, until the meat is fork-tender.

Let the brisket cool a little bit. Then, strain the sauce into a separate container. Cover the brisket tightly with aluminum foil, and refrigerate both the brisket and the sauce overnight.

The next day, preheat the over to 300°F. Slice the brisket against the grain and place in a roasting pan. Remove the fat from the surface of the sauce. Pour the sauce over the meat and heat in the oven until warm, about 30 minutes.

yiddish word of the day ✡ **simcha = celebration**

Onion Soup Mix Variation: Leave out the chile sauce and honey. Instead, in a small bowl combine 1 packet of onion soup mix, ¾ cup water, 2 or 3 whole allspice berries, ½ teaspoon garlic powder, and ¼ teaspoon dried rosemary. Pour the mixture over the brisket and bake according to the recipe.

Sweet and Sour Meatballs

The possibilities for my sweet and sour meatballs are endless! For a healthy weeknight meal, I serve them over brown rice or egg noodles, or in sub rolls. When I'm entertaining, as an appetizer I put a toothpick in each meatball and serve them on a platter. They're always gone before I have a chance to sit down. In fact, one Thanksgiving my granddaughter brought me a meatball on a toothpick. I told her that it was very good. "Don't you recognize it?" she replied. "It's your recipe!" I couldn't have been prouder at that moment. I think people love them so much because of the comforting, slightly tangy flavor. Best of all, you can make these ahead and freeze them for up to a month.

*Makes 20 meatballs,
4 to 5 servings*

1 pound lean ground beef

1 cup soft breadcrumbs

1 large egg, lightly beaten

2 tablespoons minced onions

1 garlic clove, minced

Dash of pepper

2 tablespoons water

1 tablespoon vegetable oil

²/₃ cup chile sauce

²/₃ cup grape jelly

In a large bowl, combine the beef, breadcrumbs, egg, onions, garlic, pepper, and water and mix just until combined. Be careful not to overmix, or your meatballs will be tough! Form the mixture into 1½-inch balls, about twenty to twenty-five balls in total.

In a large frying pan, heat the oil over medium heat. Add the meatballs to the pan and cook them for 5 minutes. Cover the pan, turn the heat down to low, and continue to cook the meatballs for another 5 minutes. Uncover the pan and place the meatballs on a plate. Drain the excess fat from the pan. Add the chile sauce and grape jelly to the pan and turn up the heat to medium. Cook the sauce, stirring constantly, until the jelly melts and the sauce is smooth and bubbling a little bit, about 3 minutes.

Return the meatballs to the pan and baste them with the sauce until they are well covered.

yiddish word of the day ✡ **fleshig** = **meat**

Practice Makes Perfect Dinners

In my first year of marriage, like many new brides I was eager to prepare new recipes every night for dinner. I tried to copy many of my mother's recipes, such as her pot roast, her roast chicken, and her fried lox, but somehow they never came out as good. I also tried to make new recipes, which I tore out of magazines or the newspaper, or heard about through friends. Those never seemed to taste quite right, either.

Each night we sat down to dinner and because Zadie was hungry, he ate his food with gusto. At the end of the meal I would always ask, "How was it? What did you think of what I cooked?" And Zadie would try to hide his expression. At first he would say, "It was all right. It was all right." But after a few months he became more honest.

"Well, you know, honey, it's good. But why don't you try making it again? Or try something else. Have you checked the recipe with your mother and your friends?"

Nothing is worse than when someone criticizes your cooking! "What was wrong with it?" I asked. "What was missing? Does it need more salt? More pepper? More sugar?"

"Well," Zadie replied. "I really can't pinpoint it. I'm not quite sure what it needs."

I began testing my dishes each afternoon as I prepared dinner. I tested them so much that my tongue became immune to the food and I couldn't taste it anymore! Then I ran to my mother's and asked her to taste it. She was very patient with me. We sat down and went over every step of my recipes and she asked, "Did you add garlic powder? Did you add too much onion? Not enough cinnamon?" Working together, we decided that I needed to include more garlic and spice. Still, it took time for me to adjust my taste buds and figure out how to prepare food that wasn't too bland or too strong.

It was those afternoons that taught me to be patient in the kitchen. If at first you don't succeed, try again. With a lot of time and practice you can become an accomplished and confident cook!

Chicken and Meatball Fricassee

Frica-what? Fricassee, of course. Fricassee is a classic Jewish American dish sort of like Italian ragu. Chicken and meatballs are sautéed together in a sauce made with garlic, onions, and mushrooms and served over rice or noodles. You can also spoon the mixture into puff pastry shells and serve it as an appetizer. The flavors blend together in the pan for results that are truly *geshmak*—that's Yiddish for delicious!

Makes 6 servings

Chicken

2 tablespoons vegetable oil

1 cup diced onions (about 1 onion)

1 (1-pound) boneless, skinless chicken breast, cut into 8 pieces

2 tablespoons all-purpose flour

2 cups boiling water

1/8 teaspoon paprika

2 or 3 whole allspice berries

1 bay leaf

1 large garlic clove, minced (or 1/2 teaspoon garlic powder)

1 small can sliced mushrooms or 5 fresh mushrooms, sliced

Kosher salt and pepper

To make the chicken, heat the oil in a large nonstick skillet over medium-high heat. Add the onions and cook until they are soft and golden, about 5 minutes. Add the chicken to the skillet and cook it until it is a little bit browned. Stir in the flour, then add the boiling water, paprika, allspice, bay leaf, and garlic. Stir everything to combine, then cover the skillet, turn the heat down to low, and simmer for 20 minutes.

While the chicken is simmering, **make the meatballs**. In a large bowl, combine the ground beef, egg, breadcrumbs, onions, garlic, pepper, and water. With clean hands work the mixture until it is just combined, being careful not to overwork it. Roll the mixture into twenty to twenty-five balls, each about 1 inch in diameter.

Carefully add the meatballs to the skillet with the chicken, moving the chicken pieces aside to make room. Add the mushrooms, cover, and simmer for 20 minutes more, until the chicken and the meatballs are cooked and the sauce is thick.

If the fricassee looks dry, add a little more boiling water. Season with salt and pepper and serve over rice or egg noodles.

Meatballs

1 pound lean ground beef

1 large egg, lightly beaten

1 cup soft breadcrumbs

2 tablespoons minced onions

1 garlic clove, minced

$\frac{1}{8}$ teaspoon pepper

2 tablespoons water

4 to 6 cups cooked white rice or egg noodles, for serving

Beef Tzimis

This makes a perfect one-pot meal! The dried fruit makes it deliciously sweet. Best of all, beef tzimis tastes better the day after you make it so you can plan ahead!

Makes 5 to 6 servings

1 tablespoon vegetable oil

1½ pounds beef stew meat, cut into chunks

1 small onion, diced

2 cups water

1 pound carrots, peeled and sliced into ¾-inch pieces

1 medium sweet potato, peeled and cut into chunks

6 dried apricots

6 prunes, pitted

1 tablespoon golden raisins

¼ cup freshly squeezed orange juice

2 slices of lemon

½ cup honey

¼ teaspoon kosher salt

⅛ teaspoon pepper

¼ teaspoon cinnamon

⅛ teaspoon allspice

1 tablespoon cornstarch

¼ cup water

Pour the vegetable oil in a large Dutch oven and heat it up over medium heat. Add the beef and the onions and cook until the beef is browned on all sides and the onions are beginning to soften. Add the water and bring to a boil. Put the cover on the Dutch oven, turn the heat down to low, and simmer for 1 hour, stirring occasionally.

Then, stir in the carrots, sweet potatoes, apricots, prunes, and raisins. Return the mixture to a boil, then turn the heat down to low and simmer for 30 minutes. Stir in the orange juice, lemon slices, honey, salt, pepper, cinnamon, and allspice. Simmer (with the cover on) over low heat for 1½ hours.

In a small bowl, mix the cornstarch with the ¼ cup of water until it is smooth. Stir the cornstarch mixture into the pot and simmer for 10 to 15 minutes until it has thickened and looks like gravy. With a spoon, taste and add a little more honey, lemon, or water if needed.

Note: Although this tastes better the next day, don't be tempted to freeze this because it will become mushy.

Vegetarian Tzimis

I have eaten a lot of tzimis in my day, and I've found that there are no two alike. Some are made with only vegetables and served as a side dish. My recipe is one I learned how to make while on vacation in the Catskills.

Makes 5 to 6 servings

10 cups water

5 sweet potatoes, peeled

1 pound carrots, peeled and
    cut into 2-inch pieces

6 dried apricots

1 tablespoon raisins

½ cup dried prunes (optional)

1 cup orange juice

½ cup honey

½ teaspoon kosher salt

¼ teaspoon ground cinnamon

1 teaspoon lemon juice

4 tablespoons pareve margarine

Bring the water to boil in a large pot. Add the sweet potatoes and cook for 10 minutes. Add the carrots and cook for another 10 minutes. Preheat the over to 350°F.

Drain the potatoes and rinse with cold water until cool enough to handle. Cut the potatoes into quarters and place in a baking pan with the carrots, apricots, raisins, and prunes, if using.

Combine the orange juice, honey, salt, cinnamon, and lemon juice in a bowl. Mix well and pour over the potato mixture in the pan. Stir gently. Cut the margarine into small pieces and scatter on top. Cover with aluminum foil and bake for 30 minutes. Uncover, stir gently, and bake for another 10 minutes, uncovered.

yiddish word of the day ✡ **peysekhdik = fit for Passover**

Easy Kreplach

Traditionally, kreplach (which are sort of like Jewish ravioli) are eaten three times a year: on Purim, Hoshana Raba, and at the meal before Yom Kippur Eve. Instead of making the dough myself I use Chinese wonton wrappers, which are so much easier! While beef kreplach are my favorite, kreplach are really delicious when made with ground chicken, too. Kreplach are mostly served with chicken soup. They can also be pan-fried and served as a side dish or appetizer.

Makes 10 to 12 servings

4 tablespoons vegetable oil, plus more for brushing

1 small onion, diced

2 cups cooked leftover ground roast or ground beef

¼ teaspoon pepper

1 large egg, lightly beaten

1 tablespoon matzo meal (optional)

24 to 30 wonton wrappers

Heat 2 tablespoons of the vegetable oil in a large skillet over medium-high heat. Add the onion and cook until it has softened and turned translucent. Add the ground beef and cook for a few minutes until it is heated through and is well mixed with the onions and oil. Take the skillet off of the heat and let the beef mixture cool for a few minutes.

Place the beef mixture in a food processor and pulse until the mixture is finely chopped. Pour the mixture into a bowl and stir in the pepper and the egg. If the mixture seems too wet, add the matzo meal.

Now, make the kreplach. Read the instructions carefully. I promise it's not too hard! First, spoon 1 teaspoon of the beef mixture in the center of a wonton wrapper. Next, brush the edges of the wrapper with water and fold the wrapper in half over the filling to make a triangle. Press on the edges to seal them. Then, fold the side corners together over the middle and pinch them together with a little water to seal them. Place the kreplach on a plate and cover it with plastic wrap so the kreplach won't dry out. Repeat the process with remaining wonton wrappers and beef mixture.

Now it's time to cook them. Bring a large pot of lightly salted water to a boil. Gently lower the kreplach, a few at a time, into the water. Cook the kreplach for 20 minutes, until they float to the top. Fish them out with a slotted spoon and place them on a plate. Brush them lightly with vegetable oil so that they won't stick.

When the kreplach have cooled, heat the remaining 2 tablespoons of vegetable oil in a large skillet. Fry the kreplach over medium heat until they are golden brown on both sides. Serve them hot as an appetizer or with clear chicken soup.

Stuffed Cabbage

Stuffed cabbage can seem like an intimidating dish because there are many components: the cabbage, the filling, and the sauce. Whew! It is a lot, but the results are worth it. The hardest part is preparing the cabbage. Trust me, after that it's easy. I make stuffed cabbage every fall for Sukkot, the Jewish holiday celebrating the harvest. Stuffed cabbage tastes even better the day after it is prepared, so let it sit overnight in the refrigerator if you can. It also freezes well. Don't throw out the leftover cabbage. Instead, use it to line the bottom of the pot! Serve this cabbage from the bottom of the pot as a side dish with roast chicken or meat.

Makes 6 to 8 servings

1 medium green cabbage (about 3 to 3½ pounds)

Filling

1 pound ground beef

1 large egg

¾ cup cooked white rice

1 tablespoon finely chopped onions

½ teaspoon garlic powder

1 tablespoon ketchup

Sauce

1 (6-ounce) can tomato paste

¼ cup freshly squeezed lemon juice

First, get the cabbage ready: cut off the bottom stem and remove the tough outer leaves. Place the cabbage in a large pot and cover it with water. Bring the pot to a boil over high heat. Turn the heat down to low, cover the pot, and simmer the cabbage for 10 to 15 minutes until the leaves are a little soft. Place the cabbage on a plate and let it cool a little bit, until it is easy to handle. Carefully peel the leaves from the cabbage. Trim off the bottom back of the tough stem from each leaf, keeping the leaf intact. You will need about ten to twelve total leaves. (Don't throw out the inner part of cabbage! You will need it in a minute.) If a few of the leaves tear, don't worry. Just make a patch with another piece of leaf.

To make the filling, combine the ground beef, egg, rice, onions, garlic powder, and ketchup in a large bowl. Mix everything together with a fork until it is well combined.

To make the sauce, combine the tomato paste, lemon juice, sugar, raisins, and the water in a medium bowl. Stir well to combine everything.

---

yiddish word of the day ✡ **heymish = traditional, homey, and friendly**

Cut the small, inner layers of the cabbage and arrange them over the bottom of a large pot or Dutch oven.

Now it's time to make the cabbage rolls. Place one cabbage leaf in front of you on a work surface. Spoon 1 to 2 tablespoons of the filling at the stem end of the leaf. Fold in the sides of leaf over the filling and then roll the leaf, starting at the bottom, filled end, to create a tight roll. Place the roll seam-side down in the Dutch oven on top of the cabbage leaves. Repeat with the rest of the cabbage leaves and filling.

Pour the sauce over the cabbage rolls and bring the pot to a boil. Turn the heat down to low, cover the pot, and simmer for 1½ hours. Place the cabbage rolls on a serving plate and pour the sauce from the pot over them.

¼ cup granulated sugar, or more to taste

¼ cup raisins

1½ cups water

Pepper Steak

I've always thought of pepper steak as a Chinese dish. I have found by using ketchup I can get the flavor and the taste I like for mine. I have received many compliments and have even been asked for the recipe for this variation. I like this recipe for pepper steak because it is very easy and simple to make. Be sure you serve it with plenty of white or brown rice to soak up the sauce.

Makes 6 servings

2 tablespoons vegetable oil

1½-pounds shoulder steak,
    cut into strips ½ inch wide

1 tablespoon all-purpose flour

½ cup ketchup

½ cup water

3 tablespoons soy sauce

1 beef bouillon cube

⅛ teaspoon pepper

1 large onion, sliced into thin rings

1 green bell pepper, cored, seeded,
    and sliced into thin rings

1 red, yellow, or orange bell
    pepper, cored, seeded, and
    sliced into thin rings

½ cup sliced fresh mushrooms,
    or 1 (4-ounce) can sliced
    mushrooms with liquid

Cooked white or brown rice,
    for serving

Heat the vegetable oil in a large skillet over medium heat. Add the steak strips and cook them, stirring occasionally, until they are no longer pink and beginning to brown. Place the steak on a plate.

Stir the flour, ketchup, water, soy sauce, bouillon, and pepper into the skillet and bring the mixture to a boil. Make sure the bouillon has dissolved. Return the steak to the skillet along with the onions. Cover the skillet and turn the heat down to low. Let everything simmer, stirring occasionally, for 30 minutes or until the meat is fork-tender.

Add the peppers and mushrooms and simmer for an additional 15 minutes. Serve the steak mixture over rice.

yiddish word of the day ✡ **vetsere = dinner or supper**

Cholent

Cholent is a slow-cooked stew with a rich gravy. It's very tasty and the aroma that fills your kitchen as it is cooking is wonderful! The reason cholent is so important to the Jewish people is that you can put it on the stove on Friday afternoon and cook it slowly overnight until Saturday afternoon, after the Sabbath service. Today, there is gourmet cholent, and vegetarian cholent, and sweet cholent . . . so many kinds!

Makes 5 or 6 servings

2 teaspoons vegetable oil

1 pound beef stew meat, cut into chunks

1 medium onion, chopped

½ cup dried lima beans

½ cup dried white beans

½ cup barley

3 large potatoes, peeled and quartered, or 6 small potatoes, peeled and left whole

2 tablespoons ketchup

¼ teaspoon garlic powder

1 beef bouillon cube

Kosher salt and pepper

Heat the oil in a large pot or a Dutch oven over medium heat. Add the beef and cook, stirring occasionally, until it is no longer pink, about 6 minutes. Add the onions and cook for 2 minutes. Add the lima beans, white beans, and barley. Pour enough water into the pot to cover the ingredients by about 3 inches. Cover the pot and bring it to a boil. Skim off any foam from the surface. Turn the heat down to low and simmer, covered for 1 hour.

Then, add the potatoes, and stir in the ketchup, garlic powder, bouillon, and a pinch of salt and pepper. Add more water if necessary! There should be enough water to cover all the ingredients. Bring the mixture back to a boil, then reduce the heat to low and simmer for 30 minutes. Make sure the bouillon is dissolved. Taste the cholent with a spoon and add more salt and pepper if needed. If you need to, add more water to the pot again. The ingredients should be covered by 3 inches of water.

Either cover the pot and place it in a preheated 200°F oven, or transfer the cholent to a slow cooker and cook on low heat. Cook the cholent for at least 4 to 5 hours, and up to overnight.

yiddish word of the day ✡ **tishtech** = **tablecloth**

Pitcha

Wait, don't turn the page! Yes, pitcha is a jellied dish made with calves' feet, but it's one of my favorites. My mother used to make pitcha during the week to have ready for lunch on Saturday after Sabbath services. The aroma of the garlic made my sisters and me so hungry. We would sample it while it was still hot. Sometimes, we would ladle whole bowlfuls of hot pitcha and soak it up with challah or bulkie rolls. It was so delicious, but pitcha did have one drawback—it made our breath smell like garlic! The only way to get rid of it was to chew a whole stick of gum.

Makes 12 servings

2 calves' feet, quartered

3 quarts cold water

2 onions, peeled and quartered

2½ teaspoons kosher salt

4 cloves garlic, chopped or finely minced

3 large hard-boiled eggs (optional)

⅛ teaspoon pepper, or to taste

Wash the calves' feet well and place them in a large stockpot. Add the water. Everything should be completely covered. If not, add more water. Bring the water to a boil and skim any foam that rises to the surface with a large spoon. Add the onions and salt. Turn the heat down to low, cover the pot, and simmer for 4 to 5 hours, until the meat is falling off the bones. While it's cooking, stir it frequently and skim any foam from the surface.

Transfer the meat and bones to a plate. Strain the broth through a sieve into a large bowl. Separate the meat and cartilage from the bones and throw out the bones. Mince the meat and cartilage and combine it with the garlic. Stir the meat into the broth.

Pour the broth into a 13 x 9-inch glass or plastic pan and chill in the refrigerator for 30 minutes. Slice the hard-boiled eggs, if using. When the pitcha has started to gel, layer the egg slices over the surface. If you add the eggs too soon they will sink. Return the pitcha to the refrigerator and chill until completely set, at least

12 hours. Skim any fat from the surface before serving. To serve, cut the pitcha into small squares.

Note: The meat and cartilage can be minced in a food processor. Pie plates are ideal for making pitcha. You don't want the pitcha to be too thick. Serve it in wedges like a pie.

Bubbe's Shepherd's Pie

My shepherd's pie is so tasty, you would never suspect it is made with leftovers. It is such a homey, comforting dish to have on a cold winter's night. Just add a salad for a complete meal. Ask your delicatessen or kosher butcher for "deli ends," which are very inexpensive and work perfectly in this recipe. This shepherd's pie freezes really well, so you can make it in advance and then serve it on a weeknight when you don't have time to cook.

Makes 6 servings

2 cups low-sodium beef broth or 1 beef bouillon cube plus 2 cups of water

16 ounces deli meats or deli ends, excess fat trimmed

6 to 8 ounces cooked beef, chicken, or turkey, cut into bite-size pieces

1 (12-ounce) package frozen mixed vegetables, or 1½ cups cooked leftover vegetables

5 large potatoes

2 tablespoons pareve margarine, divided

Kosher salt and pepper

Paprika

Bring the beef broth to a boil in a medium saucepan. Add the deli meats and cook them for 2 minutes. Strain the broth into a container so that there are no pieces of spices left in the broth and reserve. Then cut deli meats into bite-size pieces. Mix the cooked meat with the deli meats and set aside.

Prepare the frozen vegetables according to the instructions on the package. Set the vegetables aside.

Peel the potatoes and cut each one into 8 chunks. Place them in a large pot and add cold water to cover. Bring to a boil, then reduce the heat to a simmer and cook until the potatoes are tender, 10 to 15 minutes. Drain the potatoes and save 1 cup of the cooking liquid. Return the potatoes to the pot and add 1 tablespoon of the margarine and a pinch of salt and pepper. Mash the potatoes with a fork or a potato masher. Add a little bit of the cooking liquid to achieve a creamy consistency. You might not need the whole cup, but it's best to be on the safe side.

Spread the meat mixture over the bottom of an 8 x 10-inch oval casserole dish or a 10-inch round baking dish. Top the meat with the vegetables and pour the reserved beef broth over the top. Spread the mashed potatoes over all of the ingredients, smoothing the mashed potatoes evenly to the edges.

Melt the remaining tablespoon of pareve margarine in a small saucepan and drizzle it over the potatoes. Sprinkle the potatoes with a little bit of paprika. Using a spoon, make a small hole in the center of the potatoes to allow steam to escape. Preheat oven to 350 degrees.

Transfer the casserole to the oven and bake for 45 minutes until the potatoes are lightly browned. Let stand for 15 minutes before serving.

Stuffed Pepper Rings

These hearty stuffed peppers are perfect for dinner on a cold winter's night, especially when served with mashed potatoes. You can use all green peppers, or a mixture of green, red, and yellow. I find that cutting the bottoms off the peppers helps them stand up in the baking dish. Also, it allows more of the delicious sauce to be absorbed into the filling.

Makes 6 servings

6 medium to large bell peppers

1 pound ground beef

1 medium onion, chopped, plus 2 tablespoons minced onions

⅛ teaspoon pepper

¼ teaspoon garlic powder

1 cup cooked white rice

1 tablespoon ketchup

1 large egg, lightly beaten

3 teaspoons granulated sugar

1 (8-ounce) can tomato paste

Preheat the oven to 350°F. Cut the tops and bottoms off the peppers. Don't throw them away! Instead, coarsely chop them and set them aside. Remove the seeds from the peppers and rinse each pepper. Set them aside, too.

In a large bowl, combine the ground beef, 2 tablespoons of minced onion, the pepper, garlic powder, rice, ketchup, and egg. Mix well to combine.

Spread the chopped onion over the bottom of a 10 x 6 x 2-inch baking dish. Add the chopped pepper tops and bottoms. Carefully spoon the beef mixture into each pepper, holding the bottom so that the filling doesn't fall out. Arrange the filled peppers in the baking dish. Pour the tomato sauce evenly over the peppers and sprinkle each with ½ teaspoon sugar. Cover the dish with aluminum foil and bake for 50 to 60 minutes, until the peppers are tender.

When the peppers are done, carefully remove them from the baking dish with a spatula and place them in a large bowl or pretty serving dish. Pour the sauce left in the baking dish through a strainer, pressing on the onions and pepper to strain as much sauce as possible. Stir the sauce and spoon it over the stuffed peppers.

yiddish word of the day ✡ **hemd** = **shirt**

Short Ribs with Special Marinade

These flavorful short ribs are my favorite food to cook for unexpected guests. Both the short ribs and the sauce can be made in advance and frozen separately. Once they are defrosted, just heat up the ribs in the microwave before coating them with the sauce. As I learned as a Girl Scout many years ago, "always be prepared!" I like to serve them with rice and a green vegetable or vegetarian baked beans.

Makes 4 to 6 servings

3 to 4 pounds beef short ribs, cut into serving-size pieces

1 bay leaf

½ cup sweet and sour sauce

1 tablespoon ketchup

1½ teaspoons garlic powder

1½ teaspoons onion powder

½ teaspoon soy sauce

½ teaspoon vinegar

⅛ teaspoon pepper

Place the short ribs in a large pot or Dutch oven. Add enough water to the pot to cover the ribs completely. Add in the bay leaf. Bring the pot to a boil, turn the heat down to a simmer. Simmer the short ribs until the meat is fork-tender, about 1½ to 2 hours. Take the short ribs out of the pot and place them on a large plate.

Next, make the sauce. In a medium-size bowl, stir together the sweet and sour sauce, ketchup, garlic powder, onion powder, soy sauce, vinegar, and pepper.

Coat each short rib with the sauce. Make sure you get all the little nooks and crannies! The sauce is the best part. Place the sauce-coated short ribs back on the plate and place the plate in the refrigerator. Let them marinate for 2 or 3 hours.

Now it's time to cook your short ribs. If it's cold outside, heat up your broiler. Place the ribs on a broiler pan and broil them about 4 inches from the heat until they are brown, 8 to 10 minutes per side. Brush the ribs with extra sauce when you turn them. If it's nice outside, grill the short ribs over a very hot grill until they are nicely browned, 5 to 7 minutes a side. Brush them with extra sauce when you turn them.

yiddish word of the day ✡ **oytser** = treasure

Lamb Stew

This stew makes a hearty meal on a cold winter's day. I love the flavor and aroma of rosemary, but if you don't care for it just leave it out. You can make this stew a day or two in advance. Refrigerate the lamb and vegetables separately from the gravy. Before you reheat everything try to scrape the fat off the surface of the gravy with a spoon. It's healthier that way, too!

Makes 3 to 4 servings

¼ cup all-purpose flour

⅛ teaspoon paprika

⅛ teaspoon pepper

⅛ teaspoon garlic powder

4 or 5 lamb shanks (or 2 pounds cubed lamb's neck with bones, or 1 pound boneless lamb cut into 2-inch cubes)

2 tablespoons vegetable oil

2 potatoes, quartered

3 medium onions, quartered

3 carrots, cut crosswise into chunks

1 cup cubed yellow turnip

1 stalk celery, roughly chopped

1 bay leaf

⅛ teaspoon dried rosemary (optional)

Kosher salt and pepper

Mix together the flour, paprika, pepper, and garlic powder on a large plate. Coat the lamb pieces with the flour mixture. Make sure you get all the sides. Heat up a heavy pot or a Dutch oven. Pour in the vegetable oil. When the oil is nice and hot, add the lamb. Don't crowd the pot! If you have to, work in batches. Sear the lamb on all sides.

Add enough water to the pot to barely cover the lamb. Place the cover on the pot and lower the heat to a simmer. Cook for 1 hour. Every now and then stir the pot with a large spoon. Scrape the bottom to make sure you get all the small bits that might be stuck.

After an hour, add the potatoes, onions, carrots, turnip, and celery. Stir in the bay leaf and the rosemary (if you are using it). Bring the pot back to a boil and then lower the heat to a simmer. Cook for 30 to 45 minutes. Make sure there is enough liquid in the pot—that is what becomes the delicious gravy! If you need to, add a little more water.

After 45 minutes, check to make sure the lamb and vegetables are fork-tender. Remove the lamb and place it on a plate. Check again to make sure there is enough liquid in the pot. If not,

yiddish word of the day ✡ **shoykhet = a person who slaughters animals according to religious laws** add a little boiling water. Taste the stew and season it with salt and pepper. Use a large spoon to try and skim some of the fat from the surface of the gravy. Don't worry if you can't remove it all. Just do the best you can.

Divide the lamb between four or five shallow bowls. Add some of the vegetables from the pot to each bowl and spoon on some gravy. Serve hot.

Stuffed Breast of Veal

Stuffed breast of veal is an ideal main course for a special occasion. It takes a long time to cook, but the preparation is simple and the results are absolutely wonderful: tender, flavorful meat filled with a hearty, delicious stuffing. If you have any leftovers, you can freeze slices individually.

Ask your butcher to make a pocket on the underside of the veal for the stuffing. Make sure that he doesn't cut through the sides or the top! Also, ask him to crack the breast bones so that it will be easier to cut into serving slices.

Make sure you have metal skewers or a trussing needle and thread on hand for this recipe. You will need them to close up the pocket in the veal.

Makes 6 to 8 servings

4 tablespoons pareve margarine

¼ cup chopped onion

½ cup cornflakes

½ cup quick-cooking oatmeal

3 cups breadcrumbs (made from leftover challah or bulkie rolls)

¼ teaspoon pepper

⅓ cup chicken stock

1 veal breast (5 to 7 pounds)

Garlic powder

Onion powder

Preheat the oven to 350°F. Heat up a large frying pan and add the margarine. Add the onion and sauté until it is tender. Take the pan off the heat.

In a bowl, combine the cornflakes, oatmeal, breadcrumbs, and pepper. Stir in the onions and any margarine from the pan. Add the chicken stock and mix until everything is blended and moistened.

Stuff the pocket of veal with the stuffing. To close the opening, secure it with metal skewers or sew it with 100 percent cotton thread or twine and a trussing needle. It takes a few minutes, but it will keep all the delicious stuffing inside.

Place the veal in a large roasting pan and sprinkle it with a little garlic powder, onion powder, paprika, and rosemary, if using. Place allspice berries on top and sides of the veal breasts. Roast the veal for 30 minutes. Then, add the water to the pan and cover

yiddish word of the day ✡ **chutzpah = nerve, brazenness**

it tightly with heavy aluminum foil. Lower the oven to 325°F and cook for about 2 hours more. Check the pan often to make sure that there is enough liquid at the bottom and it's not dry. You don't want your veal to dry out! If needed, add a little more water. Baste several times while cooking. Test the veal to see if it is done. The meat should be tender when pierced with a fork.

When the veal is done, take it out of the roasting pan and place it on a carving tray. Strain the liquid "gravy" from the pan into a bowl. Skim the fat off the top with a spoon. It's easier if you put the gravy in the refrigerator for a few minutes first. Let the stuffed veal rest for 15 minutes. Carefully slice the veal so that the stuffing will stay in place. If the stuffing is dry add about 1 tablespoon of chicken broth over stuffing of each slice.

Dried rosemary (optional)

3 allspice berries

Paprika

1 cup water

London Broil or Eye Roast with Bubbe's Marinade

My marinade works great with London broil (shoulder steak) or eye roast. London broil can be broiled or grilled and also roasted. Eye roast should be roasted in the oven. Other than that, the instructions are the same! Make sure to use a meat thermometer for oven roasting medium rare. I like to prepare this dish first thing in the morning and then let the meat marinate all day. That way, it really soaks up all the flavors.

If you have any leftovers, freeze the meat and sauce separately. To reheat them, thaw the meat completely and then pop it in the microwave for a minute or two. Thaw the sauce and heat it up in a small saucepan.

Makes 4 to 5 servings

1½ to 2 pounds London broil or eye roast

¼ cup soy sauce

3 tablespoons honey

2 tablespoons white vinegar

1½ teaspoons garlic powder

1½ teaspoons ground ginger, or 1 teaspoon freshly grated gingerroot

½ cup vegetable oil

1 cup minced onions

With a fork poke several times on both sides of the meat. In a large nonreactive (not metal) bowl or self-sealed plastic bag, mix together the soy sauce, honey, vinegar, garlic powder, ginger, vegetable oil, and onions and add the meat. Place the meat in the refrigerator and let it marinate all day, or even overnight. Stir and turn it every now and then.

When it is time to cook the meat take it out of the refrigerator and let it come to room temperature. If you are making London broil, heat up your broiler or grill. Broil or grill the meat for 4 to 5 minutes on each side for medium rare.

If you are making eye roast, follow the same marinating instructions. Preheat the oven to 350°F. Transfer the meat to a roasting pan and roast it for 15 to 20 minutes per side. It should be medium rare inside; a meat thermometer, if you have one, should register 135°F, or make a small cut to check for a little pinkness.

yiddish word of the day ✡ **farputzt = dressed up**

Let the meat rest for 5 minutes. Meanwhile, pour the leftover marinade in the dish into a small saucepan. Bring it to a boil. Then lower the heat and simmer the marinade for 5 minutes. It makes a delicious sauce!

To serve the meat, slice it diagonally into thin slices. Pour the boiled marinade over the meat or serve it on the side.

Spaghetti and Meatballs

Spaghetti and meatballs is a classic Italian dish, one that I grew up with. We lived near Italian neighbors, and my mother was able to adjust their recipe into a kosher one. It tastes so much better than grabbing a jar off the shelf of a supermarket. The way that I do it may not be authentic Italian, but it saves you time and the taste is tops. It is so easy, too. I like to season mine very simply, with only onions, garlic, pepper, and sometimes a little bit of sugar for sweetness. For a real feast, serve spaghetti and meatballs with garlic bread and a green salad tossed with what else—Italian dressing.

Makes 5 or 6 servings

Meatballs

1 pound lean ground beef

1 cup soft fresh breadcrumbs

1 large egg, lightly beaten

1 garlic clove, minced

2 tablespoons minced onions

⅛ teaspoon pepper

1 tablespoon vegetable oil
   or olive oil

Sauce

1 tablespoon vegetable oil
   or olive oil

2 large onions, minced

3 cloves garlic, minced

1 (28-ounce) can diced
   tomatoes

First, **make your meatballs**. Mix the ground beef, breadcrumbs, egg, garlic, onions, and pepper in a large bowl. Make sure all the ingredients are well combined but don't mix too much or your meatballs will be tough. Shape the mixture into twenty to twenty-five balls.

Heat up the oil in a large frying pan over medium-low heat. Add the meatballs to the pan. Cook for 5 minutes on medium low then cover the pan. Cook the meatballs for 10 to 12 minutes, until they are cooked all the way through. If you're not sure, cut into the middle of one to see if it's done. Place the meatballs on a plate. Pour off the fat.

Next, **make the sauce**. Heat up the skillet again and add the vegetable oil. Then add the onions and garlic and sauté until they are very lightly brown. Add the diced tomatoes, tomato paste, and pepper. Stir everything together and turn the heat down to low. Cook the sauce for 15 minutes. If sauce is too thick add ¼ cup boiled water. Then, add the meatballs to the sauce and cook

yiddish word of the day ✡ **tokhter = daughter**

them for 20 minutes until they are nice and hot and the flavors are blended. Taste the sauce. If it is too acidic for your liking add ¼ to ½ teaspoon of sugar and cook for 1 minute more. Set meatballs and sauce aside.

Cook the spaghetti according to the directions on the package. Drain the spaghetti but save ¼ cup of the cooking water. Take the meatballs out of the sauce and place them back on their plate. Toss the pasta with the sauce a little bit at a time to make sure everything is evenly mixed. If it's a little dry, add some of the pasta cooking water.

To serve, place the pasta in a large serving dish and arrange the meatballs on top.

1 (6-ounce) can tomato paste

⅛ teaspoon pepper

¼ to ½ teaspoon sugar (optional)

1 (1-pound) package spaghetti

The Most Expensive Spaghetti and Meatballs

It shouldn't come as a surprise that food is somewhat of an obsession for my family and me. I always have a dish tucked away in the freezer just in case I need to feed my unexpected grandchildren in a hurry! And of course there is nothing I like better than to serve them a healthful meal.

In fact, a few years ago my grandson Avrom went to New York City for a television production internship with Al Roker. I was very concerned that he would forget to eat well and take care of himself. So I froze about a dozen meals, packed them individually, and sent them with Avrom to the city. Well, of course he didn't eat a single one. He was so busy, and there is so much exotic kosher food in New York that he wanted to try. When his internship was over he brought back all the frozen dinners untouched. But I didn't mind— it meant I didn't have to cook for a week!

My mother used to do the same thing. She was always packing up food and sending it to my siblings, especially my sister.

When my sister got married she moved to New York. She lived very high up in an apartment building. Since she was used to living at our house, where there were porches and windows, the city made her feel very claustrophobic. "It's like a prison," she would say on the phone. "You get up for work, get in the elevator, close the door and that's it. There is nothing to see out the window, I'm so high up I can't see anything or anyone. No trees, no grass, just other buildings staring back at me!"

On her days off she called my mother wanting to know how to make spaghetti and meatballs. My mother always explained just how to do it, but inevitably my sister would call back half an hour later with more questions. Again and again she called! Finally my mother figured out that it was because my sister was lonely. Not only did she want her food to taste just like home, she wanted to be home as well.

Fortunately my sister soon had children, and her life became very busy and full. She even learned how to make delicious spaghetti and meatballs on her own. Still, she felt they never tasted quite as good as our mother's. Sometimes, after dropping her children at school, my sister would take the quick airplane shuttle home to visit us for the day. The ride was only about an hour each way.

One time, my mother packed up a giant bowl of spaghetti and meatballs for my sister to take back with her. When my sister got to the airport, everyone was staring at her because they could smell the garlic and tomato sauce. When she got to the security check, the guard pulled out the bowl. "What is this?" he asked. So my sister had to explain how her entire family loved her mother's spaghetti and meatballs, and she had flown all the way home just to pick up dinner to take back with her. It's a story we still laugh about today.

Old-Fashioned Beef Pot Roast (Gedempte Flaish)

I love pot roast because there are so many different ways to cook it, and the results are always delicious. I give you the most basic instructions for this recipe. Just simmer the pot roast on the stovetop for a few hours until it is tender and full of flavor. Another option is to cook the pot roast in the oven: after you add the beef broth to the pot, place the pot in a 325°F oven and continue to cook for 2 ½ hours. Check often, about every 30 minutes, to make sure there is enough liquid in the pot. You can always add a little more water.

I've also made pot roast in my slow cooker: after searing the beef, transfer it to a slow cooker and add the remaining ingredients. Cook on low heat for 6 to 8 hours or according to your slow cooker instructions.

If you want to make a thicker gravy, pour the broth from the pot into a small saucepan and add ½ cup cold water and ¼ cup flour, stirring slowly until smooth, and bring the pot to a boil. Simmer the gravy for a minute or two and stir until it has thickened. It's so easy and delicious!

I always serve my pot roast with mashed or baked potatoes and a green vegetable.

Makes 8 to 10 servings

2 tablespoons all-purpose flour

⅛ teaspoon pepper

⅛ teaspoon paprika

4 pounds beef chuck roast (with or without bone)

2 tablespoons vegetable oil

3 medium onions, diced

2 cups beef broth (or 2 cups boiling water mixed with one beef bouillon cube)

Mix together the flour, pepper, and paprika in a bowl. Sprinkle the beef with the flour mixture. Make sure you get each side. Heat up the vegetable oil in a large, heavy pot or a Dutch oven. Add the beef and sear it a little bit on all sides. Carefully scrape a little of the bottom of the pot with a wooden spoon to loosen some of the browned bits. They have so much flavor!

Next, add the onions to the pot. Turn the heat down to low and simmer for 30 minutes. Add the beef broth, cover the pot, and simmer for 1 hour. Take the cover off the pot and carefully turn the beef over with tongs or two large spoons. Add the garlic, allspice berries, and rosemary (if you are using it). Cover the pot again and cook for $1\frac{1}{2}$ hours more on low simmer. Check the meat with a fork to make sure that it is cooked fork-tender.

Carefully lift the roast out of the pot and place it on a plate to rest. Strain the broth through a sieve into a large bowl. Remove the allspice berries (or bay leaf). With a strainer, mash and strain the cooked onions and, with a spoon, scrape the bottom of the strainer into a bowl with the broth. This will become the gravy that you serve with the pot roast. Give it a taste. If it is too salty, add a little boiling water.

Slice the pot roast into thick slices and pour some of the gravy over the top. Serve any extra gravy in a small bowl.

2 garlic cloves, crushed

3 whole allspice berries or 1 bay leaf

$\frac{1}{8}$ teaspoon dried rosemary (optional)

Burning My First Pot Roast

Zadie and I were married about a year after he got out of the army. We were lucky enough to be able to live in an apartment in my parents' three-tenement home. I was just learning how to cook and was very excited to have dinner ready for Zadie every day when he got home from work.

One day I decided to make a pot roast in my brand new Dutch oven, which I had received as a shower gift. I looked at a bunch of recipes and thought, "This is perfect. It will be easy. I can just put the pot roast in the oven and do other things as it cooks."

I got everything ready, chopped the onions, and put the pot roast in the Dutch oven. I placed it in the oven to cook. Then I made a few phone calls and did a few household chores. Somehow I completely forgot about it! All of a sudden I walked out of the bedroom and smelled something burning. Oh my goodness! My delicious pot roast that I wanted so badly to turn out perfect! I ran to the oven, opened it, and took the cover off the Dutch oven. The whole bottom of my pot roast was burnt. I had to use a spatula to scrape it off the bottom of the pot. What was I going to do? Zadie would be home in an hour and a half and I had no dinner. I ran upstairs to my mother's apartment.

Bubbe (left) with friends in front of the local kosher meat market

"Ma, what should I do?" I asked.

"What a coincidence," she said. "I happened to be making pot roast, too. I'll tell you what. You take mine and I'll take yours. I'll salvage it somehow. I'll cut off the burnt part and we'll manage."

And that's exactly what we did. Instead of leaving my mother's pot roast in her pot, I got out one of my best serving dishes. When Zadie came home I presented him a beautiful meal. Oh, he was so excited! "You really can cook," he said happily. I just smiled. I didn't want to lie, so I didn't say a word.

In fact, it took me ten years to finally admit, "Do you remember the first pot roast that I made? Well it really wasn't mine, it was my mother's. I burned the whole bottom of the one I made." Zadie couldn't believe it. We laughed and laughed.

Here is a tip: when you are cooking, you can't just leave things on the stove or in the oven. It's important to check your dishes and give them a stir every so often. Also, practice, practice, practice! Make dishes ahead so you can perfect the recipe. That way you will always be prepared and relaxed in the kitchen, and your meals will be delicious.

Homemade Pickled Corned Beef

I like to make food from different cultures and taste different flavors, like my version of the Irish American traditional classic corned beef and cabbage. Perfect during the winter season, this dish makes a good hearty meal and, if sliced thin, can make good sandwiches. Even when buying corned beef brisket I like to add two large cloves of crushed garlic and a bay leaf or two during cooking time to enhance the flavor more. When the corned beef is cooked I remove it from the pot without removing the liquid. Then I cut up cabbage into small pieces, add baby carrots and whole small peeled potatoes, and place those in the pot.

The stock gives the vegetables so much flavor and makes them a wonderful (and easy!) side dish. This recipe usually yields plenty of leftovers. But don't worry—leftover corned beef is even more delicious the next day.

Makes 8 to 10 servings

5 to 6 pounds beef brisket, preferably second or corner cut

½ cup kosher salt

2 tablespoons pickling spice

10 or 12 garlic cloves, crushed

4 cups cold water

Place the brisket in a large glass or ceramic dish (don't use a metal bowl). In a small bowl, mix together the salt, pickling spice, garlic, and the water. Pour the salt mixture over the brisket. The water should cover the meat completely. If it doesn't, add a little more water. Cover the dish tightly with plastic wrap and place it in the refrigerator for at least eight days and up to ten days.

When you are ready to cook the beef, take it out of the pickling liquid. Discard the pickling liquid. Place the beef in a large pot and add enough cold water to cover it completely. Slowly bring the pot to a boil. Skim off any foam that rises to the surface with a large spoon. Turn the heat down to low and simmer the beef until it is fork-tender, 3 or 4 hours. Remove the corned beef from the pot and place it on a cutting board. Cut it crosswise into slices.

yiddish word of the day ✡ **hakn a tshaynik = to talk too much, literally to chop a teakettle**

Beef Tongue with Sweet and Sour Sauce and Raisins

These days tongue has gone out of fashion. It is such a shame! I grew up eating beef tongue, and loving it, as did many people I know. It is so tender and flavorful, and there are many ways to prepare it. Some people pickle or braise tongue, but I prefer to simmer it slowly and then top it with a tangy sweet and sour sauce made with honey, raisins, and fresh lemon juice.

Makes 6 to 8 servings

Tongue

1 beef tongue (4 to 5 pounds)

1 onion, cut in half

3 garlic cloves, crushed

3 whole allspice berries

2 bay leaves

Sauce

2 tablespoons cornstarch

1½ cups water

⅓ cup honey, or more to taste

¾ cup golden raisins

¼ teaspoon freshly grated lemon zest

2 tablespoons lemon juice

1 tablespoon white vinegar

Rinse the tongue over the sink with cold water. Place the tongue in a large pot. Add enough water to cover it completely. Bring the pot to a boil and skim any foam off the surface with a large spoon. Add the onions, garlic, allspice, and bay leaves. Cover the pot but leave the lid slightly ajar to let the steam escape. Turn the heat down to a simmer and cook the tongue for about 3 hours, until it is tender when you pierce it with a fork. Check the tongue from time to time to make sure there is still enough water in the pot to cover it completely.

When the tongue is cooked, take it out of the pot and place it on a plate. Let it cool off slightly. Then, trim the "root" off the bottom of the tongue and gently remove the skin by scraping it with a fork.

To make the sauce, combine the cornstarch with the water in a small saucepan. Mix well. Add the honey, raisins, lemon zest, lemon juice, and vinegar. Bring the ingredients in the saucepan to a boil, stirring constantly. Boil the sauce for 2 minutes, until it has thickened. If it is too tangy add a little more honey.

Slice the tongue and serve it with the sauce.

yiddish word of the day ✡ **oygn** = eyes

Vegetables, Grains & Side Dishes

Don't think of this chapter as second fiddle to the previous one devoted to poultry and beef. Vegetables and grains play such an important roll in traditional Jewish cuisine. My favorites include Kasha Varnishkes, Noodle Kugel, and above all else, Potato Latkes! Even if you've never tasted Kasha Varnishkes before, you must try it. Not only does it taste good, but it is healthy as well. Boy, are you in for a real treat! A change from rice and potatoes. Today it can easily be found in the kosher section of almost any supermarket.

I'm going to show you how to make two of my favorite kugels. The first is a Noodle Kugel that is so creamy and delicious you can serve it for dessert (and sometimes I do!). The second is a Potato Kugel made with eggs and matzo meal and baked until it is golden-brown and crispy at the edges. It is the perfect side dish to complement the meal.

There is nothing like homemade latkes, especially the way that I make them. I have tried many kinds and variations but keep coming back to the original. I have received many compliments especially through email from folks who want to make it like their mothers did but didn't have the recipe. My recipe tastes like the latkes you remember when you were growing up, or if this is your first time, it will create an extra special bonus to the meal that will turn your family into fans for years to come.

Everyone has their own way of making potato latkes for Chanukah. I'm not one to say whose is best, but mine are pretty terrific. The secret is just to grate the potatoes and *don't* remove the liquid, as so many people do. Just follow my recipe, and you, too, will learn to be a latke star in your own kitchen. I fry my latkes in plenty of hot oil until they are well browned and lacy at the edges. Pass the applesauce and sour cream!

To round things out, I've also shared some new recipes that I've recently come to love, like Eggplant Lasagna with mushrooms and peppers, Twice-Baked Sweet Potatoes with cinnamon, walnuts, and dried cranberries, and a Four-Bean Salad that I always pack for picnics and is the perfect way to complete any dish.

Bubbe's Noodle Kugel

My noodle pudding is a healthy dish with old-fashioned flavor. The wonderful smells of eggs, sugar, milk, and vanilla all baking together in the oven are irresistible. You can almost taste the kugel as it cooks! Use either medium or wide egg noodles, or yolk-free noodles. You can also substitute low-fat sour cream, low-fat cottage cheese, and fat-free milk if you prefer. Of course, noodle kugel makes a delicious dessert, and you can also serve it as a delicious side dish.

Makes 8 to 10 servings

8 ounces egg noodles (half a package)

4 tablespoons margarine, melted and cooled slightly, plus more for greasing the pan

1 cup sour cream

1 cup cottage cheese

2 large eggs, lightly beaten

½ cup granulated sugar

1 teaspoon vanilla extract

1½ cups milk

Cinnamon, for garnish (optional)

Cook the egg noodles according to the package instructions. Heat the oven to 350°F. Grease a 9 x 13-inch glass baking dish with butter or margarine.

In a large bowl, mix together the noodles, margarine, sour cream, cottage cheese, eggs, sugar, and vanilla extract. This is my favorite part. It smells so delicious, it's hard not to eat it right then!

Spread the noodle mixture in the pan and pour the milk over it evenly. Sprinkle the top with a little cinnamon if desired. Bake the kugel for 1 hour, until the center is just barely set. Serve warm or at room temperature.

yiddish word of the day ✡ **luchen = noodles**

Bubbe 911

A "Bubbe 911" is when I get a phone call or email from a fan of my Internet and TV show who needs help with a dish they are preparing. For the life of me I don't know why they wait until the very last minute to call, but they always do. I try to help as many people as I can as quickly as possible, but it's hard. I do my best, but I'm only one bubbe!

One day I was at the doctor's office and my cell phone rang. I couldn't figure out who was calling. I had to excuse myself from the doctor. "I'm sorry," I said, "but I have to take this call. It's very out of the ordinary."

Well, who was on the other end? Avrom, my grandson. "Bubbe," he said frantically, "We got an email and you have to help. A woman is having company over and she needs to know if the sauce and onions go under the brisket or over the brisket!"

"Well," I said, "email her back and tell her to put the onions under the brisket and pour the sauce all over the top."

Another time, in December, right around Chanukah, we got a call at 7:30 in the morning from a woman in the south who was having a Chanukah party. She wanted to serve latkes but she had never prepared them before. She needed to know, do you use raw potatoes or cooked? "Raw, of course!" I said. I was so glad that I was able to help her out.

At Passover one year, I was sitting at my computer when I got an instant message from someone about to bake a dessert. "Help," the message said. "Every time I bake something for Passover it comes out much too dry. Do you have any tips for baking a moist cake?" Well of course I did! I sent her back my favorite Passover dessert recipe, for Chocolate-Orange Wine Cake (page 190), which is a delicious, moist, easy cake that bakes up high in the pan and keeps well. Kids especially love it because it is chocolate.

We all have our own 911 moments in the kitchen. Just remember to be calm and take a step back. Use your resources and be creative.

Kasha Varnishkes

This dish is made with kasha and bowtie pasta. Kasha can be found in the kosher food section of the supermarket. It is a whole-grain buckwheat. It's a classic European Jewish dish. It's very healthy! In fact, I once brought a little plastic container of my kasha varnishkes to the nutritionist at my senior center. She called me up and said, "Oh, that's delicious! I'm going to recommend it to all my clients."

Makes 6 to 8 servings

1 tablespoon vegetable oil

1 medium onion, diced

1 cup sliced fresh mushrooms
(or one 4-ounce can,
drained)

1 cup medium-size kasha

1 large egg, lightly beaten

½ teaspoon kosher salt

¼ teaspoon pepper

1 beef bouillon cube

2 cups boiling water

1 cup bowtie pasta

Preheat the oven to 275°F. Heat the oil in a large frying pan. Add the onions and the mushrooms and cook them until the mushrooms have softened and the onions are beginning to turn golden. Take the pan off the heat and set it aside.

In a Dutch oven (or another heavy-bottomed pot that you can put in the oven) stir together the kasha, egg, salt, and pepper. Make sure that every kernel is covered in egg. Place the pot, uncovered, in the oven for 3 to 5 minutes, just until the kasha is dry and beginning to toast. Be careful that it doesn't burn!

Meanwhile, while the kasha is in the oven, dissolve the bouillon in the boiling water.

Take the pot with the kasha out of the oven and stir in the onions and mushrooms. Add the bouillon broth and mix well. Cover the pot and return it to the oven for 30 minutes or until all of the liquid has absorbed.

While the kasha mixture is in the oven, cook the bowtie pasta according to the package instructions. Drain the pasta and set aside.

When the kasha mixture is ready, transfer it to a large bowl and mix the kasha together with the pasta.

yiddish word of the day ✡ **teler = plates**

Potato Latkes

It just wouldn't be Chanukah without potato latkes! I've given measurements for the recipe below, but don't worry too much about making sure everything is exact. If you follow my tried-and-true instructions, your latkes will be wonderful no matter what. Serve them with lots of applesauce and sour cream.

Makes about 24 small latkes

5 large potatoes

1 small onion

2 large eggs, lightly beaten

1 teaspoon kosher salt,
   or more to taste

1/8 teaspoon pepper

1/4 cup flour or matzo meal

Vegetable oil, for frying

Grate the potatoes and the onion into a large bowl. (If you want, you can cut the potatoes and onion into pieces and then blend them in a blender or a food processor.) Do not remove the liquid from the potatoes. Mix in the eggs, salt, pepper, and flour or matzo meal. Let the mixture stand for 5 minutes to thicken a little bit.

In a large frying pan, heat a layer of oil that is about 1/8- to 1/4-inch deep until it is hot, but not smoking hot. To make each latke, use a large spoon to transfer some of the potato mixture to the pan. Fry the latkes until they are well browned on both sides and crisp around the edges. Drain the latkes well on paper towels. Serve them immediately or keep them warm in an oven that you have heated up to 250°F.

Note: These can be frozen with aluminum foil between the layers and reheated in a preheated 400°F oven for 5 to 6 minutes. It makes it easier when you prepare them ahead of time and they taste very good and crispy.

Twice-Baked Sweet Potatoes

These potatoes are so tasty and full of fall flavors. The honey, vanilla, and cinnamon make them almost as sweet as dessert! My favorite part is the topping, which is a combination of walnuts and dried cranberries or raisins, plus mandarin oranges, which give the potatoes a really unique taste. This dish is ideal for Rosh Hashanah or Thanksgiving. You can assemble it through the last step a day ahead and refrigerate. Add topping when ready to use.

Makes 8 servings

Potatoes

4 medium-to-large sweet potatoes or yams

3 tablespoons pareve margarine

¼ cup honey

½ teaspoon vanilla extract

½ teaspoon cinnamon

Pinch of nutmeg (optional)

Topping

2 tablespoons chopped walnuts

2 tablespoons dried cranberries or raisins

⅓ cup peeled and diced apple

⅓ cup canned mandarin oranges, drained

Preheat the oven to 375°F.

First, cook the potatoes. Pierce each potato three or four times with a fork. Bake the potatoes for about 1½ hours, until they are soft when you touch them. Take the potatoes out of the oven and let them cool. Lower the oven temperature to 350°F.

Cut each potato in half lengthwise. With a tablespoon, scoop out the insides (don't throw them out! You'll need them in a minute), leaving about ¼ inch of potato around the inside of the skins. Be careful to keep the skins whole.

Place the scooped out potatoes in a large bowl. Add the margarine, honey, vanilla extract, cinnamon, and nutmeg (if you are using it) and mash them with a potato masher or fork until well mixed. Set aside.

In a small bowl, combine the walnuts, cranberries, apple, and mandarin oranges.

Spoon the potato mixture back into the potato skins, dividing it evenly. Top each potato with some of the walnut mixture. Bake the potatoes for 10 to 15 minutes until they are warmed through.

yiddish word of the day ✡ **sheech** = shoes

Four-Bean Salad

This bean salad is just about the healthiest dish I can think of. It's so full of fiber, vitamins, and other nutrients. Plus, it's so easy to make. It tastes wonderful alongside Bubbe's Burgers (page 82). You can make it ahead and it travels well, so it's a perfect dish for a picnic or potluck meal.

Makes 8 to 10 servings

1 (14-ounce) can red kidney beans

1 (14-ounce) can cut green beans

1 (14-ounce) can cut yellow wax beans

1 (14-ounce) can chickpeas

1 medium onion

¾ cup sugar

½ to ⅔ cup white vinegar

½ cup vegetable oil

Rinse and drain the beans over the sink, and place them into a large bowl. Peel the onion and cut it in half lengthwise through the core end. Slice each onion half crosswise into thin half circles. Add the onion to the bowl with the beans.

In a medium bowl, whisk the sugar with ½ cup of the vinegar and the oil. Taste, and add more vinegar if needed.

Toss the dressing with the beans and chill for several hours before serving.

yiddish word of the day ✡ hoizen = pants

Eggplant Lasagna

This dish makes a great vegetarian meal. It's also wonderful to have for Shavuot, the Jewish holiday that honors the Torah. Dairy dishes are traditionally served. You could also have blintzes (page 20) or Noodle Kugel (page 152).

When you are buying eggplants, make sure to choose ones that are small to medium in size. They are sweeter than the bigger ones. Preparing the eggplant for this dish involves a little extra work, but it's really worth it in the end.

Makes 5 to 6 servings

1 medium eggplant, or two small ones (about 2 pounds total)

Kosher salt

4 tablespoons olive oil

1 large onion, diced

1 large bell pepper, any color, diced

8 ounces white mushrooms, sliced (optional)

1 large egg

1 cup breadcrumbs or matzo meal

1 (24-ounce) jar tomato-basil pasta sauce

8 ounces shredded part-skim mozzarella cheese

Peel the eggplant and cut it crosswise into ½-inch-thick slices. Place the eggplant slices in a colander and sprinkle them with salt. Let the eggplant stand for 30 minutes. This lets the moisture drain out of them. Don't worry, they won't taste too salty.

Meanwhile, preheat the oven to 350°F. Heat 1 tablespoon of the olive oil in a large nonstick pan. Add the onions, peppers, and mushrooms (if you are using them) and cook until they are softened and beginning to brown, 5 or 6 minutes. Transfer the onion mixture to a bowl.

Rinse the eggplant and press the slices lightly between paper towels. Lightly beat the egg in a bowl. Spread the breadcrumbs on a plate. Dip the eggplant slices first in the egg mixture and then in the breadcrumbs or matzo meal. Transfer them to another plate.

Add another tablespoon of the olive oil to the pan and heat over medium-high heat. Working in batches and adding more olive oil as needed, cook all of the eggplant slices until lightly golden, 2 to 3 minutes.

Spoon a thin layer of tomato sauce in the bottom of a 9 x 13-inch baking pan, and spread it out evenly. Layer half of the eggplant slices over the sauce, and then half of the onion mixture. Repeat with the remaining eggplant slices and onion mixture. Pour the rest of the sauce over the top and sprinkle with the mozzarella. Cover the pan with aluminum foil and bake for 45 minutes. Remove the foil and bake for 5 minutes more, until the cheese is bubbly and beginning to brown.

Let the lasagna rest for 15 minutes before serving.

Potato Knishes

My knishes are smaller than the ones you usually see in restaurants or delicatessens, but they are filled with homemade flavor. These days knishes are filled with all kinds of ingredients, but I think traditional potatoes and onions are best. The taste combination is a classic. These knishes are so comforting.

Makes 20 to 24 servings

Dough

2½ cups all-purpose flour

1 teaspoon baking powder

½ teaspoon kosher salt (optional)

2 large eggs

⅔ cup vegetable oil, or melted pareve margarine

2 tablespoons water

Potato Filling

6 tablespoons pareve margarine

1 cup chopped onion

2 cups mashed potatoes

1 large egg

½ teaspoon kosher salt

¼ teaspoon pepper

1 egg, lightly beaten (for brushing tops of knishes)

For the dough: Sift the flour, baking powder, and salt, if using, together in a bowl. In another large bowl, beat the eggs with the vegetable oil and water. Add the flour mixture to the egg mixture and give it a good stir until everything is well blended. Place the dough on a floured countertop. Using clean hands, knead the dough until it is no longer sticky. Place the dough in a bowl that is lightly greased with vegetable oil. Cover the bowl with plastic wrap, and let it rest in a warm place for 1 hour.

Meanwhile, **make the potato filling**. Heat the margarine in a skillet over medium heat. Add the onions and cook until they are softened and starting to brown. Remove the skillet from the heat and set aside. In a large bowl, beat the potatoes, egg, salt, and pepper with an electric mixer until well mixed. Add the onions and beat until everything is well combined.

Preheat the oven to 375°F and grease a large baking sheet.

When the dough has rested, it's time to make the knishes. First, divide the dough in half and roll each into a 9 x 5-inch rectangle. Using a drinking glass or a cookie cutter, cut out circles of dough that are 3 to 4 inches across. Scoop 1 tablespoon of potato filling

yiddish word of the day ✡ **khazeray = junk food**

into the center of a circle of dough. Lightly dampen the edges of the dough with water and fold the dough in half over the filling to form a half-moon shape. Pinch the edges to seal them and transfer the knish to the prepared baking sheet. Repeat the process with remaining dough circles and potato filling.

Brush the knishes with the beaten egg and bake for 35 minutes, until they are browned.

Three Generations of Bar Mitzvahs

Back when I was growing up, girls didn't have Bat Mitzvahs like they do today. But my husband, Zadie, had a Bar Mitzvah. When I asked him about it recently, he didn't hear me.

"Zadie," I said. "Tell me what your Bar Mitzvah was like."

"What?" he asked.

"Your Bar Miiittttzzzvah!"

"What?"

"You need to change your hearing aid!" I yelled. Zadie believes you should keep using something until it's absolutely used up, so he really gets his money's worth when it comes to batteries. He has always been very economical. That's just the way his generation was brought up. When he finally changed his batteries, he described his Bar Mitzvah.

"It was 1935. My Bar Mitzvah was at the smallest shul (orthodox synagogue) in town. I read my Torah portion, and then they had a Kiddush (a blessing recited over wine). The following day was a Sunday, and we had a big party at my house with lots of friends and family from out of town. We served delicatessen: corned beef, pastrami, salami, potato salad, cole slaw, sliced rye bread, sour pickles, mustard, and soda." It was a simple affair, but an important one that Zadie will always remember.

Years later, when it was time for our son's Bar Mitzvah, things were very different. Things weren't so simple anymore! Several hundred people were invited, so my mother and I started preparing far in advance. We didn't have enough freezer space, so we rented a large freezer at a cold storage locker a few miles out of town.

For a month before the Bar Mitzvah, we baked sponge cakes and honey cakes and brought them out to the locker and froze them. A week before the big day, we bought a huge bucket of salt herring and made picked herring and chopped herring. We also made a lot of chopped liver. The Friday morning before the Bar Mitzvah, we brought all the food to the kitchen at the synagogue so that the food would have a chance to thaw and be ready Saturday afternoon after the service.

On Saturday night, we had a big party for about 100 friends and family members. Fortunately, we didn't have to do all the cooking ourselves for that! Instead, we hired a local kosher caterer. Hors d'oeuvres, like meat knishes, cocktail frankfurters, mini potato pancakes, vegetables and dip, sliced pineapple, and melon were passed around. The main course was a delicious chicken, and for dessert we had a special Bar Mitzvah cake in the shape of an open Torah scroll. A well-known singer from the area provided the entertainment. It was a very happy evening and everyone had a great time, but it wasn't all that elaborate. We did most of the work ourselves.

Most recently was our grandson's Bar Mitzvah. He did a beautiful job and he studied very hard, so I guess he deserved a fancy party. But it seemed a little over the top to me! Everyone was all dressed up for synagogue. After the service, there was a dairy luncheon of bagels and cream cheese with lox, herring, and whitefish salad, and noodle kugel—all the trimmings.

Later that evening, there was an even more elegant party at the synagogue social hall. It was decorated in blue and white, with fresh flower centerpieces. Everything was coordinated and nothing was missing. Zadie and I felt very proud of our grandson. We sat together and took in the overwhelming sights and sounds of the party. By coincidence, it was our fiftieth wedding anniversary, and they surprised us with a beautiful cake. There was a band so big it seemed like an orchestra. It played all kinds of music—Yiddish, Jewish, and rock 'n' roll. There was also an emcee who played games with the young children, and CDs were given out as party favors. It certainly was a special night, one that I will always remember.

When I think about these three generations of Bar Mitzvahs, the important thing was not how much money was spent, how many guests there were, or how fancy the party was. The important thing was that we were all there, celebrating together as a family.

Potato Kugel

Everyone loves potato kugel. The truth is it's really simple! The secret to achieving a sensationally crispy crust is to brush a little of the oil on all sides of the empty baking pan and heat the pan in the oven for about four minutes before pouring in the potato mixture. Remember to be careful when taking the hot pan out of the oven. Try it. I promise you will never make potato kugel another way again.

Makes 6 to 8 servings

5 large baking potatoes, peeled and diced

1 medium onion, peeled and diced

3 large eggs, lightly beaten

⅓ cup matzo meal

1 teaspoon kosher salt

⅛ teaspoon pepper

4 tablespoons vegetable oil

Preheat the oven to 350°F. Grease well a 9 x 9-inch baking dish or a 2-quart casserole dish.

Place the potatoes, onions, and eggs in a large bowl and toss to combine. Working in batches, purée the potato mixture in a blender or food processor. Transfer the purée to a large bowl, add the matzo meal, salt, pepper, and vegetable oil, and give everything a good stir until it is well mixed.

Place the prepared baking dish in the oven and allow it to heat for exactly 4 minutes. Remove it from the oven (wear oven mitts—it's hot!) and pour in the potato mixture. Return the dish to the oven and bake for about 1 hour, until the kugel is golden brown.

yiddish word of the day ✡ **licht = candles**

Challah Stuffing

Everyone loves stuffing! It's a shame so many people eat it only once a year, on Thanksgiving. I give my traditional stuffing a Jewish twist by using challah breadcrumbs. To make them, cut slices of challah into chunks and toast them in a 225°F oven until they are dry and crispy. Then, use a box grater or a food processor to make them into crumbs. Using challah adds extra taste to the stuffing, making it good and delicious. I like to serve it with roast chicken, turkey, or beef, with plenty of gravy.

Makes 4 to 6 servings

3 cups challah breadcrumbs

½ cup cornflakes

½ cup quick-cooking oatmeal

¼ teaspoon pepper

⅛ teaspoon garlic powder optional)

4 tablespoons pareve margarine

1 medium onion, chopped

½ cup low-sodium chicken broth

Preheat the oven to 325°F. Grease a 1½-quart casserole dish.

In a large bowl, combine the challah breadcrumbs, cornflakes, oatmeal, pepper, and garlic powder (if you are using it).

Get a frying pan nice and hot over medium heat. Melt the margarine in the pan and then add the onions. Cook, stirring, until the onion is tender. This will take 8 to 10 minutes.

Scrape the onion mixture into the bowl with the breadcrumbs. Mix everything together well with a large spoon. Then, add the chicken broth a little bit at a time. Stir after each time you add chicken broth. You want your stuffing to be nice and moist but not too sticky or wet. You might not need all of the stock, or you might need a tiny bit more. That's okay.

Pour the stuffing into the casserole dish and spread it out evenly. Make sure you get to the corners! Cover the dish with two layers of aluminum foil. Place the stuffing in the oven and bake for 30 minutes.

Take the stuffing out and take off the aluminum foil. Fluff it up a bit with a fork. If it seems too dry, sprinkle a little chicken stock over the surface of the stuffing and fluff it up a little bit more. Serve hot.

yiddish word of the day ✡ **kuzin (male) or kuzine (female) = cousin**

Breads & Desserts

When it comes to ending an enjoyable meal, you can never go wrong with a dessert. They are filled with homemade flavors and wonderful memories! Think of Honey Cake, matzo-apple kugel, sponge cake, and Passover Mocha Nut Bars. By now, you should know that I enjoy cooking. When I'm baking Milchig Bulkelach, also known as cinnamon rolls, the house smells so good, and it feels like all is right with the world. Plus, as a bubbe, I just love to share my baked treats with family and friends. Who can say "no" to a plate of warm brownies or a slice of apple kugel?

Desserts come in two categories: everyday treats and those reserved for special occasions. I am going to share my favorites from each category. When my children were growing up they were always so hungry when they returned home after a long day at school. Who could blame them with all that running around they do? I always tried to have a delicious snack ready for them as soon as they came through the door. Since I was working, it had to be something quick and easy. That's how I came up with recipes like Vanilla-Chocolate Brownies, Chocolate Ricotta Cake (which uses store-bought cake mix), and of course my famous Jelly Jammies, which are a simplified rendition of my mother's traditional Jewish strudel.

On the more elegant side, there are recipes for Holiday Cookies and a Chocolate-Orange Wine Cake that is sure to be a showstopper at a Passover Seder. I always serve it to rave reviews, and no one ever guesses how easy it is to prepare. My mother's Pineapple Sponge Cake is a dessert that I serve regularly to company. It looks so pretty on the plate, and the pineapple flavor is always a sweet surprise. She used to make it with a handheld mixer and it took so much elbow grease! These days I use my electric mixer and it is so quick and simple.

There are plenty of traditional Jewish favorites, too, like mandel bread (my version is marbled with chocolate and includes a little bit of kosher wine), Honey Cake made with cloves and coffee, and *kichlach* (that's Yiddish for puffed cookie) sprinkled with sugar.

If there is one thing I've learned in all my years as a bubbe it is that life is too short to skip dessert! I hope you will give all of my recipes a try. Each one is a cherished family favorite. I'm sure they will be in your family, too.

Marble Mandel Bread

This recipe has been in my family for years, and it's one of my all-time favorites. Mandel bread is very similar to Italian biscotti. It's delicious with a cup of coffee or tea. Here is a baking tip: this dough can be very soft and sometimes it's tricky to form it into a log or loaf shape. I found that old-fashioned metal ice cube trays make excellent mandel bread baking pans. Just spread the dough in the pan and it comes out perfectly! My mandel bread looks so pretty when it's sliced and you can see the chocolate swirls inside. I like to add a sprinkle of cinnamon sugar on top for an even sweeter taste.

*Makes 2 loaves,
16 to 20 slices*

3 cups all-purpose flour

3 teaspoons baking powder

¼ teaspoon kosher salt

3 large eggs

1 cup plus 1 tablespoon
    granulated sugar

½ cup vegetable oil

1 tablespoon Concord grape
    wine or vanilla extract

1 tablespoon cocoa powder

1 tablespoon cinnamon

Make sure the rack is in the center of your oven. Preheat the oven to 350°F. Grease two 9 x 5-inch loaf pans with nonstick spray or line them with nonstick aluminum foil.

In a medium bowl, sift together the flour, baking powder, and salt.

In a large bowl, beat the eggs with an electric mixer until they are nice and frothy. Slowly add 1 cup of the sugar and continue beating until the mixture is thick and lemon colored, about 2 minutes. Beat in the vegetable oil and the wine. Slowly beat in the flour mixture just until it's combined. Be careful not to overmix!

Now make the chocolate batter. Spoon one-third of the batter into a little bowl. Add the cocoa powder and stir until it's well mixed.

Divide the white batter that remains between the prepared pans and spread it evenly. Spoon half the chocolate batter over the white batter lengthwise down the middle of each pan.

In a small bowl, stir together the remaining tablespoon of sugar and the cinnamon. Sprinkle half the cinnamon mixture over the batter in each pan. Transfer the pans to the oven and bake for 25 to 30 minutes, until the mandel bread is dry to the touch and when a toothpick inserted into the center comes out clean.

Cool the pans on a wire rack for 15 minutes, then remove the mandel bread from the pans and cut crosswise into thick slices using a serrated knife.

Note: I suppose another wine might work, but I've never tried it with any other wine.

The Family Circle

Rose was Zadie's first cousin. Zadie came from a large family. There were six children in Zadie's father's family. Part of the family lived in New York and the other ones lived in other various areas. As a result there were many, many first cousins, plus their children. A few of the first cousins decided that it would be a good idea if we could have a family circle where we could get together regularly. The local family got together once a month. Those from out of town managed to come in once a year, or whenever possible. We worked very hard. We had to hire a hall because our homes were too small to have all of us meet together. We took turns bringing refreshments, and we also collected dues to pay for the children's Chanukah parties and also for our yearly banquet. We had a secretary record notes. We had a full set of officers. Every year we voted for the officers. We ran our family circle like any other organization.

One time when we got through with the meeting and went downstairs to the car, Zadie opened the car and he looked in the back and there was a man stretched out sleeping across the whole back seat. He smelled strongly of liquor. Zadie drove to the police station, which was nearby, and got two policemen to come out and drag the man out of the car. A cell phone would have come in very handy at that time.

There were many different foods but one that stood out was Rose's Marble Mandle Bread (page 168). It was a little different than the ordinary mandle bread, and it had a very good flavor. I have served it many times and I have received many compliments for it.

Matzo Apple Kugel

This sweet baked pudding is a little bit like bread pudding, only it's made with matzo in place of the bread. This is one of my favorite traditional Passover recipes, but it can be eaten at any time of the year. Everyone loves the warm flavors of apples and cinnamon. You can serve this kugel warm or at room temperature, topped with a spoonful of sour cream (use light sour cream—it's healthier!). Usually, it's a dessert, but for an extra-special treat that everyone will love, you can serve it as a side dish.

Makes 4 to 6 servings

3 plain matzo

2 large tart apples, such as Granny Smith, peeled and thinly sliced

3 large eggs, lightly beaten

½ cup granulated sugar

¼ teaspoon cinnamon

2 tablespoons pareve margarine, melted, or vegetable oil

½ teaspoon freshly grated lemon zest

Preheat the oven to 350°F. Grease a 1¾-quart casserole dish, or a 9 x 9-inch baking dish.

Break the matzo into large pieces, place them in a bowl, and cover them with water. Soak the matzo until they are soft but not too mushy. Drain the water from the bowl and add the apples, eggs, sugar, cinnamon, margarine, and lemon zest. Mix well with a large spoon.

Pour the batter into the prepared baking dish and bake for 35 to 40 minutes, until the kugel is lightly browned.

Note: To make a nice presentation, save 10 to 12 slices of apple and lay them on top before baking.

yiddish word of the day ✡ **bruder = brother**

Matzo Meal Rolls

I always made Matzo Meal Rolls for the children when they were young and also my grandchildren. They are easy to digest and satisfying. I like to make them early in the morning or in the evening and have them ready for breakfast or lunch. I serve the rolls with butter and a slice of cheese or cream cheese and jam. You can even use cream cheese and a slice of lox. They are so easy to make.

Makes 8 to 10 servings

2 cups matzo meal

1 tablespoon sugar

1 teaspoon kosher salt

1 cup water

½ cup vegetable oil

4 eggs

Preheat oven 375°F. Use a cookie sheet and grease well. Mix matzo meal, sugar, and salt together in a small bowl. In a small saucepan bring water and oil to a boil. Add matzo meal mixture to saucepan and mix well. To this mixture add one egg at a time, mixing well after each egg. Let the mixture rest for 15 minutes. Oil your hands and form the dough into twelve rolls. Place on greased cooking sheet 2 inches apart. Bake 45 to 50 minutes until golden brown.

Honey Cake

Honey cake is traditionally served at Rosh Hashanah, the Jewish New Year. For the holiday meal, we also eat apples dipped in honey to ensure a sweet year ahead. Honey cake is also eaten all year, especially at the Shabbos Kiddush. It tastes a bit like gingerbread. I like to add ground cloves, but you can use nutmeg, allspice, or cinnamon if you prefer. Coffee may seem like a strange ingredient, but trust me! It really brings out the flavors.

Makes one 9 x 9-inch baking pan serving 8 to 10

3 cups all-purpose flour

2 teaspoons baking powder

1 teaspoon baking soda

½ teaspoon ground cloves or ¼ teaspoon nutmeg and ¼ teaspoon allspice

4 large eggs

1 cup packed dark brown sugar

1 cup honey

¼ cup vegetable oil

1 teaspoon vanilla extract

½ cup strong brewed coffee

Preheat the oven to 325°F. Grease a 9 x 9-inch baking pan or spray it with nonstick spray. Dust the pan with flour and tap out the excess.

In a medium bowl, sift together the flour, baking powder, baking soda, and cloves. In a large bowl, using an electric mixer, beat together the eggs and brown sugar until they are blended. Beat in the honey, vegetable oil, and vanilla extract. First beat in a little coffee, then a little of the flour mixture, then a little more coffee, then a little more flour until everything is mixed.

Pour the batter into the prepared pan and bake for 55 to 60 minutes, until a toothpick inserted in the center comes out with a few moist crumbs attached. Let the cake cool for 10 minutes, then remove the cake from the pan and cool completely on a wire rack.

yiddish word of the day ✡ **sholem-bayes** = peace

Pineapple Sponge Cake

Sponge cake is one of the most traditional desserts around. You can serve it for Shabbos, yontif (holidays), or any other time you like. My mother had a cousin who used to drink five to six glasses (not cups, glasses!) of tea at one time. My mother would serve him a large slice of sponge cake to go along with his tea. I still have the large bowl and handheld beaters my mother used to make sponge cake, but these days, I use an electric mixer! You can make this sponge cake ahead and freeze it for up to three months.

Makes one 10-inch cake, serving 8

1½ cups all-purpose flour

1 teaspoon baking powder

6 large eggs, separated

½ teaspoon kosher salt

1½ cups sugar, divided

½ cup pineapple juice

1 tablespoon freshly squeezed lemon juice

Whipped cream and strawberries, for serving (optional)

Preheat the oven to 325°F. Sift together the flour and baking powder in a medium bowl. In a large bowl, using an electric mixer, beat the egg whites and the salt until soft peaks form, about 1½ minutes. Gradually beat in ¾ cup of the sugar to the egg whites and beat until stiff peaks form but not dry, about 1½ minutes.

In a separate large bowl, beat the egg yolks for 1 minute until thick and fluffy. Then beat in gradually ¾ cup sugar. Turn off the mixer and add the pineapple juice and the lemon juice. Turn the mixer on low speed and gradually add the flour mixture to the yolk mixture and beat just until blended.

Carefully fold the egg white mixture into the yolk mixture until just blended. Don't worry if there are still a few streaks of egg white—it's important not to overmix! Spoon the batter into a 10-inch tube pan and bake for 1 hour until the cake is golden and springs back when pressed lightly.

Turn the cake upside-down over a wire rack and allow it to cool completely. Loosen the cake with a spatula or knife and remove the pan. Serve plain or with whipped cream and strawberries.

yiddish word of the day ✡ **gut nakht = good night**

The Real Story Behind My Mixer

Many of the people who email me about my Internet cooking show want to know about my mixer. How old is it? How long have I had it? Where can they buy one just like it? Unfortunately they can't buy the same one. They don't make them like that anymore. It's a collectable, an antique. But I will tell you the story of the day I bought it.

We were having company over for dinner. I was making my delicious Pineapple Sponge Cake for dessert. My flour was sifted and I was just starting to beat the eggs with my mixer when it went kaput. The whole thing just stopped all together. No matter what I tried I couldn't get it to work. What was I going to do? I didn't have time to get it fixed. I decided to run to the store and buy a new one. I left the bowl of cake batter on the counter, grabbed some money for the bus, picked up my three-year-old son, and dashed out the door.

When I got to the store, all the mixers were so expensive! Even the simple handheld kind cost way more than I wanted to pay. I was about to give up when I spotted a stand mixer on sale. I bought it and hurried for home.

Back in my kitchen, I was hurried and stressed. I was rushing, and I couldn't figure out how to put my new mixer together. I didn't know how to get the beaters to fit into their slots. Finally, after many attempts, I pieced everything together. I threw together the rest of the cake ingredients and slid the pan into the oven. My son watched the whole thing, wide-eyed to see his normally pulled-together mother so out of sorts.

Well wouldn't you know it, when I took the cake out it was as flat as a pancake. I left the batter on the counter for so long that the eggs I had beaten deflated. My sponge cake hadn't risen at all. I threw the whole thing in the garbage pail.

Of course, when Zadie got home, the first words out of my son's mouth were, "Mommy made a cake and then she threw it in the garbage can!" I'll never forget that moment. You think a child is too young to know what's going on, but in reality they understand everything!

Holiday Cookies

When my grandchildren were very young, I looked forward to baking and decorating these cookies for Chanukah. It is my mother's recipe. I make the dough ahead and store it in the refrigerator. Then we cut out the cookies together and decorate them once they come out of the oven. If you have cookie cutters in special shapes, like a dreidel or the Star of David, use them. If not, a drinking glass will do. Serve these for dessert after a meal of my Potato Latkes (page 155). Delicious!

Makes 20 to 24 cookies

3 cups all-purpose flour

2 teaspoons baking powder

¼ teaspoon kosher salt

2 large eggs

4 ounces (1 stick) pareve margarine

1 cup granulated sugar

1 large egg white, lightly beaten

Candy sprinkles, cinnamon sugar, and colored frosting for decorating

Make sure the rack is in the middle of the oven. Preheat the oven to 375°F. Line a large baking sheet with parchment paper.

In a medium bowl, sift together the flour, baking powder, and salt.

In a large bowl, beat the eggs and margarine until light and fluffy with an electric mixer. Then beat in the sugar. Gradually add two-thirds of flour mixture to the egg mixture and beat until just incorporated. Stir in the last third of the flour mixture by hand, using a spatula or a large wooden spoon. If the dough seems a little too soft, you can add a few more tablespoons of flour.

Place the dough on a work surface and knead it slightly. Divide the dough into three equal parts. Wrap two of the pieces in plastic wrap and place them in the refrigerator to chill.

Lightly sprinkle your work surface with flour. Using a rolling pin, roll the third piece of dough out to ¼ to ⅛ inch thickness. Cut into shapes with cookie cutters. Place the cookies on the prepared baking sheet. Lightly brush them with the egg white and top with decorations (except for the frosting—that comes later!).

yiddish word of the day ✡ **schtern = star**

Bake the cookies for 8 minutes, until they are set and the edges are golden brown. Allow the cookies to cool for 5 minutes on the baking sheet, then transfer them to a wire rack to cool completely. Repeat the process with remaining pieces of dough.

When the cookies have cooled completely, decorate with frosting and serve.

Passover Mocha Nut Bars

Just because it's Passover, it doesn't mean you have to pass over dessert. These bars have no flour in them, but you would never guess it. They are light, cakey, and delicious. The instant coffee granules add a hint of mocha flavor. If you are serving a large group, you may want to double the recipe and bake it in a 9 x 13-inch pan. Since you can't use baking powder or baking soda during Passover, make sure to sift the matzo cake meal, coffee granules, and salt well. It helps to keep them soft and chewy.

Makes 16 brownies

2 ounces bittersweet chocolate

½ cup vegetable oil

½ cup matzo cake meal

¼ teaspoon kosher salt

1 tablespoon instant coffee granules

2 large eggs

1 cup granulated sugar

½ cup chopped walnuts

Preheat the oven to 325°F. Grease a 9 x 9-inch baking pan with oil, or spray it with nonstick spray.

Melt the chocolate in a small bowl in the microwave. Then stir in the vegetable oil and let it cool for a few minutes.

In a medium bowl, sift the matzo cake meal, salt, and instant coffee granules.

Combine the eggs and the sugar in a large bowl and beat with an electric mixer on medium-high speed until they are nice and frothy. Add the chocolate mixture and continue to beat until everything is well mixed. Slowly beat in the sifted matzo cake meal mixture, just until it is well blended.

Pour the batter into the prepared pan. It's a pretty thick mixture, so be sure to spread it well to the edges. Sprinkle the walnuts over the top of the batter. Bake the bars for 25 to 30 minutes, until it is just set and a toothpick inserted into the center comes out with a few moist crumbs attached. Cut the bars into squares while they are still warm.

yiddish word of the day ✡ **mandlin = almonds**

Frozen Blueberry-Tofu Pudding

Tofu in dessert? Who ever heard of such a thing? Actually it's really good, and so much healthier for you! My blueberry pudding makes a delicious, light end to a summer meal. You can use whatever kind of juice you like in this recipe. There are so many options at the supermarket these days! Sometimes I like to make it with a special juice blend, like apple-raspberry.

Makes 4 to 6 servings

1 (12-to 16-ounce) package firm tofu

1 (10-ounce) package frozen no-sugar-added blueberries, or 1 pint fresh blueberries

1 large banana, ripe and frozen, cut into chunks

1 tablespoon fresh lemon juice

1 teaspoon almond extract

¼ to ½ cup honey or maple syrup, to taste

½ cup orange, pineapple, apple, or raspberry juice

2 peaches, peeled and sliced

Cut the tofu into small pieces. Place the pieces in a blender with the blueberries, banana, lemon juice, almond extract, honey, and juice and blend until the mixture is smooth.

Divide the blended mixture between four to six glass dessert dishes, place peach slices on top of each pudding, and cover each dish with plastic wrap. Place the dishes in the freezer for 30 minutes or longer.

yiddish word of the day ✡ **shvester = sister**

A Great Honor

The Torah is the five books of Moses and is the foundation of the Jewish religion. It is a scroll made from animal skin hand written with a feather pen by a specially trained scribe called a sofer. It takes around two years to complete due to the fact that each Hebrew letter must be perfect. If any of the letters are smudged or do not look right it can change the meaning of the word, which would make the Torah not permissible to use in the synagogue. A synagogue needs multiple copies of the Torah to make it easier to read different sections on the Sabbath. Not very often does a synagogue or a temple have the opportunity to bring in another Torah. Sometimes the Torah gets a little worn, and someone will donate a new Torah.

When a new Torah is dedicated there is usually a great ceremony involved. The last few lines of the Torah are outlines of each letter. Many noted members of the synagogue are given the honor to fill in these letters under the guidance of the sofer. It is a great honor to be asked to fill in one of these letters with the feather pen.

One time our synagogue received a new Torah and Zaide was given this honor. At the Rabbi's home everyone gathered around a table where the Torah was laid out. After everyone filled in the final letters, the Torah was lifted for everyone to see and was then covered with its cloth covering. Everyone went outside where there was a procession from the Rabbi's house to the synagogue. Everyone was dancing and singing on the way to the synagogue. During the procession many people went up to the Torah to kiss it. This is the traditional way to give honor to the Torah. At the synagogue the Torah was placed in the ark with other Torahs. Finally there was a big meal celebrating the completion of the Torah.

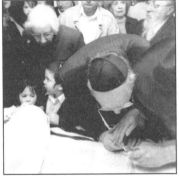

Zadie adding some of the last letters to the Torah scroll

Treasure Cake

This no-bake pudding cake is a terrific treat that I have been making for years, ever since my children were younger and their little friends stayed for lunch. You can use vanilla sandwich cookies for a summer beach version and the chocolate ones for a wintertime version. You could also serve it for Chanukah. After all, it is made with chocolate coins (gelt)!

Makes 4 to 6 servings

4 ounces cream cheese, softened

½ cup confectioners' sugar

2 tablespoons unsalted butter, softened

1 (1.7-ounce) package instant vanilla pudding mix

1¾ cups milk

1 (12-ounce) container refrigerated whipped topping

1 (16-ounce) package chocolate sandwich cookies

12 to 15 jelly beans

6 to 9 chocolate coins, foil removed

First, place the cream cheese, confectioners' sugar, and butter in a medium bowl and beat for 2 minutes using an electric mixer on low speed. In another bowl, beat the vanilla pudding mix with the milk. Combine both mixtures in a large bowl and gently fold in the whipped topping. Refrigerate the mixture until it is nice and chilled.

Next, place the chocolate sandwich cookies in a food processor and pulse until they are coarsely crumbled.

Spread one-third of the chocolate cookie crumbs in the bottom of a parfait dish or pretty serving bowl. Top the cookie crumbs with one-third of the pudding mixture. Scatter half the jelly beans and half the chocolate coins over the pudding. Repeat with another one-third of the cookie crumbs, one-third of the pudding, and the remaining jelly beans and chocolate coins. Then add the last layer of cookie crumbs and pudding. Refrigerate the cake until you are ready to serve it.

Jelly Jammies

These days, everyone has fancy kitchen equipment like miniature food processors and spice grinders. But when I need to chop nuts, as I do for this recipe, I just put them in a plastic sandwich baggie and roll a soup can across them. My Jelly Jammies have become so famous I have to keep a continuous supply in my freezer for guests. Fortunately, they couldn't be easier to prepare. I like them best made with strawberry jam, but feel free to use your favorite. These make a perfect afternoon pick-me-up with a cup of coffee or tea. Here is a tip: I hate washing pans! If you do, too, try lining yours with nonstick aluminum foil. When your Jelly Jammies are done, you can just throw the foil away—no cleanup required!

Makes 16 servings

¾ cup strawberry jam

1 medium tart apple, such as Granny Smith, peeled and coarsely grated

2 teaspoons freshly squeezed lemon juice

1 teaspoon freshly grated lemon zest

4 teaspoons chopped walnuts

⅛ teaspoon cinnamon

2 tablespoons golden raisins

1½ cups all-purpose flour

½ teaspoon kosher salt

½ teaspoon baking powder

4 ounces (1 stick) pareve margarine, softened

Preheat the oven to 400°F. Spray a 9 x 9-inch baking pan with nonstick spray or line the bottom and sides of the pan with nonstick aluminum foil.

In a medium bowl, stir the strawberry jam, apple, lemon juice, lemon zest, walnuts, cinnamon, and raisins until combined. Set it aside. In another medium bowl, sift together the flour, salt, and baking powder.

In a large bowl, beat the margarine and the sugar with an electric mixer until they are nice and light and fluffy, about 2 minutes. Beat in the egg and the vanilla extract. Slowly add the flour mixture and beat, scraping the sides as you go, until it is well mixed and forms a dough.

Spread two-thirds of the dough into the bottom of the prepared pan. Spread the jam mixture over the dough. Using your hands, gather tablespoon-size pieces of the remaining dough and flatten them into little disks. Place the dough pieces over the jam filling.

(They won't cover the filling entirely, but don't worry; it's supposed to be that way. The dough will spread.) Bake the Jelly Jamies for about 25 minutes, until the filling is bubbling and the dough is golden brown.

Cut them into 16 squares while still warm. They are hard to cut when completely cool.

Note: This recipe easily can be doubled. Just use a 13 x 9-inch baking dish and bake 25 to 30 minutes.

½ cup granulated sugar

1 large egg

1 teaspoon pure vanilla extract

Jelly Jammies

When my children were old enough to go to school for a full day I got a part-time job to supplement our income. Even though I worked during the day, I liked to have a homemade snack ready for my children when they got home. After all, they were still quite young, and they got very hungry.

My children (and just about everyone else) loved my mother's strudel. However, preparing traditional Jewish strudel is a lot of work! You have to make the dough, let it rest, then roll it out. Oy! Who has time for all that? But the filling my mother used in her strudel was actually a quite simple mixture of jam, apples, lemon juice, walnuts, cinnamon, and raisins. I decided to see if I could make a simpler version that would be a perfect after-school snack.

What a success! Who knew it would become my signature recipe? My children loved the treats so much, but they didn't know what to call them. "Ma, what's the name?" they asked. "I don't know," I said. "I just made them up." Since there was a lot of jam in them, they started calling them Jelly Jammies and the name just stuck. Now my whole family knows about Bubbe's Jelly Jammies. In fact, I have to keep a supply in the freezer at all times, just in case someone comes over for a surprise visit.

But I didn't just serve them to my family. Whenever there was a school bake sale, I made Jelly Jammies. They always sold very fast and went over big! It was even popular at meetings that I attended. I haven't found another recipe that comes close to mine—except my mother's strudel, which takes so much longer to make. I've given the recipe to so many people. Now all my neighbors make it for the holidays. At work, we exchanged recipes during our coffee break. When I brought in my Jelly Jammies everyone raved.

Every fall, when strawberry preserves go on sale at the supermarket, I generally end up buying twelve to twenty-four large jars of jam. To be honest, I don't buy them all at once.

I make two or three trips because I don't want the people at the back of the line to see me buying up all the jam! But I'm a bubbe, and I have to be prepared.

The weekend after Thanksgiving, all the cousins and nephews and nieces get together from out of town for a yearly reunion. I always make enough Jelly Jammies to be sure that we don't run out. Since they are pareve, they can be eaten with anything. They are just the thing with a cup of coffee. Children can eat six of them in one sitting!

It seemed only natural to make Jelly Jammies for the first episode of *Feed Me Bubbe*. In a way, you could say that they launched a brand new career for me. I never would have believed that posting cooking videos on the Internet would become so popular and make me a world-renowned bubbe—especially at my age. If a fortune teller told me I wouldn't have believed them.

Around the holidays I get orders for Jelly Jammies from all my family members. They bring them to all their holiday parties. It just goes to show that if you take your time to develop a really delicious signature dish, it will always shine among the other offerings. I hope you will make my Jelly Jammies for your next party, too.

Indian Pudding

When my daughter visited Durgin-Park restaurant in Boston, she came home and asked me if I knew what Indian pudding was. It was on the menu and she wanted to try it, but it wasn't kosher. (See Trying New Things, page 187.) This one is kosher. The warm, spicy flavors of the molasses, cinnamon, and ginger combine with buttery cornmeal to make a perfect, homey dessert. I like to serve it topped with scoops of vanilla ice cream.

Makes 6 servings

¼ cup cornmeal

2½ cups milk (regular or fat-free), divided

½ cup dark molasses

¼ cup granulated sugar

¼ teaspoon kosher salt

¾ teaspoon cinnamon

¼ teaspoon ground ginger

1 large egg, lightly beaten

4 tablespoons unsalted butter, diced

Preheat the oven to 300°F. Grease a small casserole dish or an 8 x 8-inch glass baking dish. Combine the cornmeal and 1¾ cups of the milk in a double boiler or in a large heatproof bowl set over a pan of simmering water. Cook over medium-high heat, whisking occasionally until the mixture is very thick but still pourable. I'd say this takes 20 to 30 minutes.

Remove the cornmeal mixture from the heat and whisk in the molasses, sugar, salt, cinnamon, ginger, egg, and butter. Whisk until the butter is melted and the mixture is smooth.

Pour the cornmeal mixture into the prepared dish. Pour the remaining ¾ cup of milk over the top. Bake the pudding for 2½ to 3 hours until it is golden brown and the center is set and no longer jiggles. Let the pudding cool slightly before serving.

Trying New Things
(My Daughter's Trip to Quincy Market)

During the summer my daughter attended day camp for a month. One day, she came home with a note stating that they were going on a field trip to Quincy Market in Boston. It gave an itinerary. It said they were going to visit the birthplace of America: Paul Revere's house, Faneuil Hall, and Durgin-Park. I packed my daughter a lunch, plus a bathing suit and towel for the park. I thought maybe they would go swimming.

Well, that night when my daughter got home she was very upset. "Durgin-Park isn't a park!" she said. "It's a restaurant that is over 175 years old!"

"What?" I said. "What kind of a restaurant is called a park?"

"It's historic. It has long, old wooden tables, and the menu is full of old-fashioned New England dishes," my daughter said. "We had our homemade lunches sitting on the benches in Quincy Market and after we were done we went to Durgin-Park to learn about the history of the restaurant and early New England cuisine." They got to ask the restaurant manager questions, like what is Indian pudding, and did the Indians make it? "Do you know what Indian pudding is?" she asked me. "I'd like to try it, since we couldn't try it there because it wasn't kosher."

Needless to say I was quite surprised. All this time I thought she was going swimming in the park. The next day I went to the library and checked out a book of recipes that told all about Indian pudding, which is made with molasses and cornmeal. My daughter and I made it together, and it is still one of my family's favorite recipes.

Sometimes keeping kosher seems hard, but it isn't really. Most recipes can easily be adapted. There are so many easy substitutions, like pareve margarine for butter, or tofu or vegetables for meat. It makes me feel good to experiment with new recipes and cuisines and find ways to make them fit a kosher lifestyle. Trying new things and developing new tastes is what life is all about!

Vanilla-Chocolate Brownies

These brownies are irresistible. First there is a layer of chocolate, then a layer of vanilla, and it's all topped off with creamy chocolate frosting. Kids love them, so this is a great recipe to make for a bake sale or for a birthday party at school. To vary the recipe, sprinkle the batter with chopped walnuts before baking. Or, leave out the frosting and simply dust the brownies with confectioners' sugar once they have cooled.

Makes 20 to 24 brownies

Brownies

2 ounces unsweetened chocolate

1 cup solid vegetable shortening

2 cups granulated sugar

4 large eggs

2 cups all-purpose flour

½ teaspoon kosher salt

½ teaspoon vanilla extract

Frosting

2 ounces unsweetened chocolate

1 cup granulated sugar

¼ cup milk

½ teaspoon vanilla extract

1 tablespoon unsalted butter

Preheat the oven to 350°F. Grease a 13 x 9-inch baking dish or spray it with nonstick spray and flour the pan.

To **make the brownies**, melt the chocolate in a bowl in the microwave. Set the chocolate aside to cool slightly.

In a large bowl, beat the vegetable shortening and the sugar together with an electric mixer until they are well mixed. Add the eggs one at a time, beating to combine after each addition. Beat in the flour, salt, and vanilla extract just until mixed. Transfer half of the batter to a medium bowl and stir in the melted chocolate.

Spread the chocolate batter in the bottom of the prepared pan. Spread the vanilla batter on top of the chocolate batter. Bake for 30 to 35 minutes, until a toothpick inserted into the center comes out with a few moist crumbs attached.

Now it's time to **make the frosting**. First, melt the chocolate in a bowl in the microwave. Transfer the chocolate to a medium saucepan and add the sugar, milk, vanilla extract, and butter. Bring the mixture to a boil, stirring constantly. Boil for 1 minute and remove the pan from the heat. Spread the frosting over the brownies while they are still warm.

yiddish word of the day ✡ **meydl = girl**

Eggless Chocolate Cake

This is a quick and easy chocolate cake that never fails to please. Serve it after a dinner of perfect Roast Chicken for a classic, soul-warming, home-cooked meal.

Makes one 8-inch round cake, 6 servings

1½ cups all-purpose flour

1 cup granulated sugar

3 tablespoons cocoa powder

1 teaspoon baking soda

½ teaspoon kosher salt

6 tablespoons vegetable oil

1 tablespoon white vinegar

1 teaspoon vanilla extract

1 cup water

Confectioners' sugar

Preheat the oven to 350°F. Grease an 8-inch round cake pan. Sift the flour, sugar, cocoa, baking soda, and salt in a large bowl. Whisk in the vegetable oil, vinegar, and vanilla extract until smooth. Add water and stir until smooth. Transfer the batter to the prepared pan and bake for 35 to 40 minutes, until a toothpick inserted in the center comes out with a few moist crumbs attached. When completely cooled, dust with confectioners' sugar.

yiddish word of the day ✡ freylekh = happy, cheerful

Chocolate-Orange Wine Cake

Today, we know it's time for Passover because supermarkets start stocking up on products like matzo, coconut macaroons, and sweet kosher wine. But it wasn't always so easy! Preparation started every fall. My mother bought several baskets of Concord grapes to make wine for Passover. She made it in a crock (cask) that easily fit in the space between our cast-iron stove and the kitchen wall. My job was to take the grapes off the stems and wash them. The grapes would soak in water, sugar, and yeast in the crock until they were fermented, and my mother would later follow the procedures for making the wine, which took some time. Now it is much easier. We can buy Passover wine almost anywhere. It reminds me of my mother whenever I make this cake. How hard she worked to prepare for Passover.

Makes one 10-inch cake, 10 to 12 servings

8 large eggs, separated

1½ cups granulated sugar

¼ cup freshly squeezed orange juice

Freshly grated zest of 1 orange

2 tablespoons kosher for Passover cocoa

¼ cup kosher for Passover concord grape wine

¾ cup matzo cake meal, sifted

Preheat the oven to 350°F. Lightly grease a 10-inch tube pan with a removable bottom.

In a large bowl, beat the egg yolks and the sugar with an electric mixer until they are thick and pale yellow. Add the orange juice, orange zest, cocoa, and wine and beat just until blended. Gently stir in the matzo cake meal.

Wash and dry your beaters. Then, in another large bowl, beat the egg whites until they are stiff but not dry. Have patience! This takes a few minutes. Carefully fold the egg whites into the batter. Pour the batter into the prepared pan and bake for 50 to 60 minutes, until a toothpick inserted in the center comes out clean. Cool the cake completely on a wire rack.

yiddish word of the day ✡ **nosh = snack**

Chocolate Ricotta Cake

Back when I was growing up, there was no such thing as boxed cake mixes. I think they are so convenient, but sometimes they need a little something extra to give them that homemade flavor. The ricotta topping on this cake is so creamy and delicious. I use part-skim ricotta because it's healthier. This recipe is really simple, so it's a great one to make no matter what your skill level.

Makes one 13 x 9-inch cake, 12 servings

1 (18.25-ounce) box chocolate cake mix

3 cups (24 ounces) part-skim ricotta cheese

1 teaspoon vanilla extract

¾ cup granulated sugar

3 large eggs

Confectioners' sugar

Preheat the oven to 350°F. Grease a 13 x 9-inch baking pan. Dust the pan with flour and tap out the excess.

Prepare the chocolate cake mix according to the directions on the back of the box. Spread the batter in the prepared pan and set aside.

Place the ricotta cheese, vanilla extract, sugar, and eggs in a large bowl. Beat with an electric mixer until the mixture is well combined. Spread the ricotta mixture over the chocolate cake batter and bake for 1 hour, until a toothpick inserted in the center comes out clean.

Cool the cake on a wire rack, then dust with confectioners' sugar. Cut the cake into squares before serving.

yiddish word of the day ✡ **Shabbos = Saturday**

Sour Cream Pie

This creamy pie is one of my favorite comfort-food desserts. The graham cracker crust is so easy. No tricky pie dough required! The secret is to leave the pie undisturbed in the oven as it cools. It helps to keep the pie nice and fluffy. Serve slices of the pie topped with crushed strawberries, or plain. Either way, you can't go wrong.

Makes 12 to 15 servings

Crust

1¼ cups graham cracker crumbs

4 tablespoons unsalted butter (or 2 tablespoons butter and 2 tablespoons margarine), melted

2 tablespoons granulated sugar

½ teaspoon cinnamon

Filling

2 large eggs, separated

½ cup granulated sugar

1 pint low-fat sour cream

½ teaspoon vanilla extract

Preheat the oven to 325°F. First, **make the crust**. In a bowl, combine the graham cracker crumbs, melted butter, sugar, and cinnamon. Save ⅓ cup of the mixture for the topping and press the rest into the bottom and sides of a 9-inch pie plate.

Next **make the filling**. In a large bowl, beat the egg yolks and sugar with an electric mixer until they are nice and light. Add the sour cream and beat until smooth. Beat in the vanilla extract.

In a separate bowl, beat the egg whites until they are stiff. Carefully fold the egg whites into the sour cream mixture. Be careful not to deflate your egg whites! Don't stir it too much.

Pour the filling into the pie plate and sprinkle with the remaining ⅓ cup of the graham cracker mixture.

Bake the pie for 20 minutes, then shut off the oven and leave the pie inside until it has cooled.

Sugar Kichlach

Kichlach is Yiddish for "a puffy cookie." These kichlach are a bit like sugar cookies, but the addition of three eggs make them puffy. They are crispy and crunchy and inside empty and dry. These cookies are the perfect snack with a cup of tea. You will typically find kichlach served with a Shabbos Kiddush after the services are over.

Makes 30 to 36 cookies

3 large eggs, room temperature

½ cup vegetable oil

1 cup all-purpose flour, sifted

¼ teaspoon kosher salt

3 tablespoons granulated sugar

Preheat the oven to 325°F. Grease a cookie sheet.

In a large bowl, beat the eggs until they are nice and light and fluffy. Add the oil, flour, salt, and 1 tablespoon of the sugar and beat until mixed well. Drop teaspoons of dough on to the cookie sheet, spacing them three inches apart. Sprinkle the dough with the remaining 2 tablespoons of the sugar. Bake for 20 to 30 minutes, until the cookies are lightly browned and the edges are puffed.

yiddish word of the day ✡ **gaas = radio**

Coming to America

My family is originally from Russia. My mother's mother and one of her brothers were killed in a pogrom (a violent military riot) during World War I. My mother's house was small and food was limited. She, being the oldest, was responsible for cleaning the house and taking care of her siblings. One day, she found a small piece of faded, yellowed paper on a high shelf in a kitchen cabinet. Written on the paper was the name of an uncle, and his address in America.

My mother decided to write to her uncle and tell him about what had happened. Maybe he could help her get a passport. Since it was the early 1920s, the mail was very slow. It took a long time before she received an answer. Finally, she got a letter saying that her uncle was sending her a ship's card that would allow her to come to America. But she had to go to Warsaw and wait for her number to come up in the quota.

My mother told her father what she was planning to do. At first he was upset, but he understood that the best way for her to help the family was to go to America. It was the land of opportunity. She could send money home, and maybe one day the rest of the family could join her. "Go straight to America and to your uncle living there," he said.

It was very dangerous to travel. My mother had a girlfriend in Warsaw who might help her. All the arrangements had to be made in secret. One night she left with nothing more than the shirt on her back. She had to walk for miles and travel across barbed wire. Her shirt was torn. How she managed she doesn't know. She just kept going.

Bubbe's mother made a dinner in appreciation of her uncle (center) bringing her to America

Finally, she reached Warsaw and found her friend. Her friend said, "What did you come for? I barely have enough food to eat for myself. If I can't take care of myself how can I help you?" But my mother was determined. She found a job as a seamstress. She lived in Warsaw for two years. On the weekends, she would go to the wharf and gaze out at the big ships. She couldn't imagine that she would ever be on one, on her way to America.

At last my mother's number was called. The voyage to America took two weeks. From Ellis Island in New York, she took a train to the small town where her uncle lived. He and his wife and son welcomed her with open arms. She found work in a knitting mill and spent some time living there. Then she met her husband, my father, and got married.

Life in America was better, but money was still scarce. Whatever extra dollars she had, she sent to her father in Russia hoping that eventually one of her brothers or sisters could come over. She sent food packages, too. Years went by, and then World War II hit. My mother's sisters were sent to Siberia. She never heard from one of her brothers or his children again. Long after the war, my mother was able to locate two of her sisters. They were alive and living back in their hometown. But they were old and frail and unable to travel.

I consider that little piece of paper my mother found to be a miracle. Even though she was never able to afford to bring her brother and sisters over from Europe, she raised a beautiful family with beautiful grandchildren. If she had never found her uncle's address, who knows if she would have even lived to have a family, or reached America—a place to dream about with freedom for all.

Jelly Roll

This was one of my children's favorite snacks with a glass of milk when they came home from school. They always liked the crisp edge pieces best, especially when they were cut off the cake straight out of the oven and still warm.

Makes 10 to 12 servings

1 cup all-purpose flour

1 teaspoon baking powder

¼ teaspoon kosher salt

3 large eggs

1 cup granulated sugar

½ cup seedless raspberry jam, warmed

Preheat the oven to 375°F. Line a 15 x 10-inch baking sheet with nonstick aluminum foil. (In a pinch, you can also use a 13 x 9-inch baking pan.)

Sift together the flour, baking powder, and salt in a bowl. In another bowl, beat the eggs and sugar with an electric mixer until they are very thick. Fold in the flour mixture. Pour the batter into the pan and spread it evenly. Bake the cake for 12 minutes, until a toothpick inserted in the center comes out clean.

Spread a clean dishtowel out on the counter and dust it with confectioners' sugar. Turn the cake over onto the towel and remove the pan. Trim the edges off the cake and save them for snacking. Using the end of the towel roll up the warm cake until cool, then unroll the cake, spread carefully with warm jam, and use the end of the towel to gently push against the cake to roll it up. Make sure that you do this quickly. The warmer the cake the easier it is to roll, and the less likely it is to break.

Let the cake cool completely and then place it on a serving plate seam-side down. Cut slices as thick as you like.

yiddish word of the day ✡ **vakatsye = vacation**

Apple Cake

When I'm in doubt about what kind of cake to bake, this apple cake usually pops into my mind. It's one of my family's favorites. It's so easy and versatile. You can serve it for dessert, for brunch, or as a snack. In the chilly fall months it's perfect with a mug of hot cocoa.

Makes 10 to 12 servings

2 cups all-purpose flour

2 teaspoons baking powder

¼ teaspoon kosher salt

4 ounces (1 stick) pareve margarine

1 cup plus 1 teaspoon sugar

⅔ cup water

1 teaspoon vanilla extract

2 large eggs

2 cups sliced apples

1 teaspoon cinnamon

Preheat the oven to 350°F. Grease a 9 x 9-inch baking pan.

In a small bowl, sift together the flour, baking powder, and salt. In a large bowl, beat the pareve margarine with an electric mixer until it is creamy. Add 1 cup of the sugar a little bit at a time and beat until it is fluffy. Slowly beat in the water. Then beat in the flour mixture and the vanilla extract. Add the eggs one at a time. Beat well after each one.

Pour half of the batter into the prepared pan. Arrange half of the apples over the batter. Mix the leftover teaspoon of sugar with the teaspoon of cinnamon in a little bowl. Sprinkle half of the cinnamon-sugar mixture over the apples. Pour the rest of the batter into the pan. Arrange the rest of the apples over the top, and sprinkle with the remaining cinnamon-sugar mixture. Bake the cake for 40 minutes, until a toothpick inserted in the center comes out clean.

Let the cake cool slightly in the pan. It can be served warm or at room temperature.

yiddish word of the day ✡ **levana = moon**

Apple Cinnamon Bread Kugel

Bread kugels are not only delicious and comforting, they are also a great way to use up leftover bread. I always have a loaf of challah in the house, but sometimes we don't get around to eating all of it before it starts to get a little stale. That's when I know it's time to make this dessert. Bread kugels puff up really high in the oven and then sink back down as they cool off. Don't worry if yours looks a little deflated in the end—it's supposed to be that way. I love to serve a plate of this topped with a little sour cream.

Makes 5 to 6 servings

3 medium apples

2 or 3 cups cubed challah bread (it doesn't need to be exact)

2 large eggs

2 tablespoons margarine

1 cup milk

⅓ cup granulated sugar

1 teaspoon vanilla extract

1 teaspoon cinnamon, plus more for sprinkling

1 tablespoon golden raisins (optional)

Sour cream, for serving (optional)

Heat up your oven to 350°F. Grease an 8 x 8-inch baking pan or a 1½-quart casserole dish.

Peel the apples, core them, and cut them into quarters. Then, cut each quarter into thin slices. Set aside.

Place the challah cubes in a bowl and cover them with cold water. Let them soak for a minute. Meanwhile, beat the eggs in a mixing bowl. Squeeze the water out of the challah and add it to the bowl with the eggs.

Melt the margarine in a small saucepan or in the microwave. Add it to the bowl with the eggs and challah along with the milk, sugar, vanilla, 1 teaspoon of cinnamon, and raisins (if you are using them). Add the sliced apples and mix well just until everything is nicely combined.

Pour the mixture into the prepared baking dish. Now, sprinkle the top with a little extra cinnamon—it adds flavor and looks pretty, too! Bake the kugel for 50 to 60 minutes. When it's done it should be lightly browned on top.

yiddish word of the day ✡ **shtetl = small town**

Easy Strawberry-Walnut Rugelach

Given the choice between cookies or rugelach, I'll choose rugelach almost every time. Rugelach are small, rolled pastries that look like tiny croissants. They can be filled with all sorts of delicious mixtures, but my favorite combination is strawberry jam and walnuts. Unfortunately, making the traditional dough for rugelach takes a long time and a lot of hard work. I use store-bought piecrusts in place of the dough. You can whip them up in about half an hour, and I promise nobody will know the difference. It can be hard to find kosher frozen piecrusts. I get mine from Trader Joe's. However, it is a dairy piecrust.

Makes 16 pastries

Two (9-inch) unbaked frozen or refrigerated piecrusts (thawed completely if frozen)

⅓ cup strawberry jam

⅛ teaspoon cinnamon

⅛ teaspoon freshly grated lemon zest

⅛ teaspoon freshly squeezed lemon juice

⅓ cup finely chopped walnuts

1 tablespoon golden raisins

First, grease a cookie sheet and set it aside. Next, spread the piecrusts out flat on the counter.

Now mix the jam, cinnamon, lemon zest, and lemon juice together in a bowl. Using a pastry brush, spread half of the mixture over the surface of each piecrust. Sprinkle both piecrusts with the walnuts and raisins.

Using a sharp knife, cut each piecrust into eight wedges. Carefully roll up each wedge, starting from the outside. Be careful to roll tightly and pinch the point at the end of each wedge to seal them. Place all the rolls on the prepared cookie sheet, leaving ½-inch space between each one. Curve each roll slightly into a crescent shape. Refrigerate the rolls for 15 minutes.

Meanwhile, heat up your oven to 350°F. When the rolls have chilled, place them in the oven and bake for 25 to 30 minutes until they are lightly golden brown. Cool them completely before serving.

yiddish word of the day ✡ **sholem-aleykhem = hello**

Hamantaschen

Purim is a very happy and fun holiday for old and young alike. It's an exciting holiday and everybody lets loose from old to young with costumes and parties and you name it! It all comes from the history of King Achashverosh, who was the king of Persia, his beautiful queen, Esther, her uncle Mordechai, and Haman who was the villain. Haman wanted to take over the kingdom, causing a lot of commotion and problems, but thanks to Queen Esther and as a result of her smart thinking, the Jews were saved.

I love Purim, not only because it is a real time to celebrate, but also because we get to eat delicious hamantaschen. Hamantaschen are little pastries filled with a poppy seed or fruit mixture. Their three-cornered shape is meant to look like Haman's hat. Sometimes hamantaschen are made with regular cookie dough. I think they are so much better when made the traditional way, with a yeast dough. Prepared poppy seed and fruit filling are available in many markets. The brand I like is called Solo. Or, if there is a kosher bakery in your neighborhood, ask if you can buy some of their filling.

Makes 15 to 20 yeast dough hamantaschen

2 (¼ ounce) packages active dry yeast

¼ cup lukewarm water

1 cup milk

¼ cup vegetable oil

½ cup sugar

1 teaspoon kosher salt

4 to 5 cups all-purpose flour

2 large eggs, plus one large egg yolk

Place the yeast in a small bowl and pour the water over it. Stir them together a bit with a spoon, then set the bowl aside and let the yeast "bloom" until it looks frothy. This should take about 5 minutes.

Meanwhile, pour the milk into a small saucepan and scald it over medium-high heat. Pour the milk into a large bowl and add the vegetable oil, sugar, and salt. Give the mixture a good stir with a wooden spoon and then let it cool for a few minutes, until it is lukewarm.

Next, add 2 cups of the flour to the milk mixture and mix well. Then, add the two whole eggs and the lemon zest and mix until they are incorporated. Add the yeast and mix that in, too.

Now, start adding more flour, a little bit at a time, just until the mixture forms a soft dough. You might not need all 4 or 5 cups, but it's good to have it on hand just in case!

yiddish word of the day ✡ **zingen** = to sing

Turn the dough out onto a countertop dusted with flour. Knead the dough until it is smooth and satiny, about 5 minutes. If the dough becomes too sticky, sprinkle it with a little more flour and keep kneading.

Place the dough into a greased bowl and turn it over once to grease the top. Cover the bowl with plastic wrap or a dishtowel and let it rise until it has doubled in bulk, about 2 hours.

Preheat the oven to 350°F.

Using a floured rolling pin, roll the dough out on a floured countertop until it is about ⅛ to ¼ inch thick. Use a drinking glass or cookie cutter to cut the dough into 3- or 4-inch circles. Gather up all the scraps, reroll them, and cut out more circles. Keep rerolling and cutting the dough until there isn't enough left!

Scoop up a heaping tablespoon of filling and place it into the center of each dough circle. Pinch the edges together in three places (at the top, and twice at the bottom) to create a triangle shape. Repeat with the remaining dough circles and filling.

Place the hamantaschen on a baking sheet and let rise until doubled in bulk, spacing them an inch apart. Combine the egg yolk in a small bowl with a little bit of water, and brush it over the tops of the hamantaschen. Bake the hamantaschen for 20 minutes, until they are lightly golden brown. Cool them on a rack before serving.

1 teaspoon freshly grated lemon zest

Store-bought poppy seed or fruit hamantaschen filling

Stewed Bartlett Pears with Apples and Cinnamon

Many years ago Zadie and I built a house on a lot that was owned by a dentist. The dentist's hobby was horticulture. As a result, we had a plum tree, a raspberry patch, and beautiful lilac bushes. Best of all, there was a tree in the front yard that produced Bartlett pears. The first year we lived there, the tree produced so many pears that I didn't know what to do with them. They grew so fast! It seemed like if I picked a basket full one day, more had grown back the next. I gave pears to family, friends, and even the mailman. The neighborhood children even began calling me "the pear lady."

I knew I had to find some good recipes for pears. I learned how to stew them, freeze them, and bake them into pies. This simple dessert was my absolute favorite way to prepare them. It is so easy, juicy, and delicious. As time went by the pear tree started to rot and during one storm the whole tree fell down. I still consider that pear tree a part of our family. I only wish my grandchildren had been able to taste the fruit. Then they would have been able to share in the history and memories. I will never forget my time as the pear lady.

Makes 6 to 8 servings

6 firm-ripe Bartlett pears

2 medium cooking apples, such as Macintosh

1/3 to 1/2 cup granulated sugar

1/8 teaspoon cinnamon

1 3/4 cups water

Peel the pears and cut them in half lengthwise. Cut down both sides of the stem so that you can pull it out easily. Cut around the cores and remove those, too. Peel the apples, core them, and cut them into quarters. Mix the sugar and cinnamon together in a small bowl.

Place the pears and apples in a large pot and add the water. Cover the pot and slowly bring it to a boil. Boil gently until the pears are just barely tender, about 5 to 10 minutes.

Add the sugar-cinnamon mixture to the pot and stir everything together gently. Bring the pot back to a boil and cook for 10 minutes more. Remove the pot from the heat and let the pears and apples cool in the cooking liquid.

yiddish word of the day ✡ tantsn = to dance

You can eat the fruit warm served straight from the pot, or you can chill it in the refrigerator. The fruit can also be frozen in the cooking liquid for later use.

Bubbe's Favorite Yiddish Songs

My audience always asks me questions about my past, wanting to get a better picture of what they may be missing out on having never been exposed to the traditions that are disappearing today. This made me think of my time when I used to go to Yiddish theater with my parents. It was a very special occasion that I always looked forward to. The bright lights, actors, and beautiful songs bring tears to my eyes even when I think about it today. I had a great time reliving memories with Avrom listening to all of the classic Yiddish songs and was surprised at how much he was taking in as we listened to each song and discussed its history. I want you to be able to have the same experience as me so I have listed out for you my favorite Yiddish songs, what they are all about, and the special connection that I have with them. While you are cooking and want to make it more of an experience, take a moment to find these songs and listen to them. You won't be disappointed.

"Chasene Valse" (Wedding Waltz): This song is also known as the "Anniversary Waltz." This was the song Zadie and I chose for our wedding. It is a very important song to us, and the words are beautiful and have great meaning. In the future, I hope that my grandchildren will play this song at their weddings.

"Oyfn Pripetchik": There is a fire burning in the fireplace, and the house is nice and warm. The Rabbi is teaching the little children the Alef-Beis (alphabet). The song is about the children learning by the warmth of the fire. This is a reminder of how I got my own Yiddish and Hebrew education growing up. I went to the home of my Rabbi, who had the exact same setup in his living room and dining room. It just so happens I was the only girl being taught with forty boys in the class, which included Zadie.

"My Yiddishe Mama": This is a song that is all about a Jewish mother and how she was so pretty and so attentive to her children. The phrase has been used for many years in the expression "a Jewish mother." The Jewish mother is known to be very protective of her children and very dedicated to her family. The song is sung by a girl who tells about what kind of mother she has. She is singing about a Jewish mother. This song became popular not only in Yiddish but translated into English as well. When I hear this song it brings memories and tears to my eyes and also makes me think of myself as a grandmother and a mother and my daughters as a mother to their children.

"Rozinkes Mit Mandlen": This song, which translates into English as "Raisins and Almonds," is a Jewish lullaby that I have sung to my children and my grandchildren. The lyrics say that under the baby's crib there is a little goat and the baby and the goat will grow together and they will sell raisins and almonds. The baby and the little goat are friends. I like it because the melody is pretty and the ending is very good when it says "shlof," meaning "sleep," telling the baby to "sleep baby sleep."

"Az Der Rebe Elimeylekh": The Rabbi was very happy and singing and wanted to sing and dance. So he sends for two fiddlers the first time around. Then he sends for other musicians and continues. Before he adds each musician you repeat the musicians he started with and increase the speed of the melody. This makes it very easy to get mixed up, and when the children were small we sang this together and we would always have a good laugh because we always lost track of the musicians. We couldn't sing it at such a fast pace the way the professionals can do it.

"Tum Balalaika": This is a song that makes me happy and hum along with the tune. It's all about a fellow who wants to date a girl but he doesn't know how to approach her. He asks the girl many different questions. One of the questions is what can cry without tears? The girl answers, "love and a heart."

"Breevele der Mammen": A mother is asking her son, who went to America, to send a little note to let her know that he is all right and to please keep in touch with her. This song makes me very sad and brings tears to my eyes when I think of many children today who become adults, go their own way, and never realize that their parents who raised them always care and that it is very seldom they receive a note or telephone call from their children who have moved away.

"Papirosn": This Yiddish song was very popular during the time of Yiddish theater. It is about a little orphan boy who is trying to sell cigarettes and it's raining and the cigarettes get wet. Nobody is buying them and he doesn't know how he is going to get enough money for food. It is a sad yet meaningful song with warm feelings. I first heard this when I went to Yiddish theater with my parents. I am grateful that they took me whenever Yiddish theater would come to our town. It reminds me of the time when my father lost his job and times were tough.

Klezmer Freyleckh: This style of music involves toe-tapping beats, and when it is played it's hard for you to sit still. This is true especially at weddings. When the children were very young and we couldn't go outside because of the snowstorms, it was wonderful entertainment for all of us to put the records on the phonograph and dance around the house.

Nigun: This is melody that uses no words and is replaced with various sounds. Some are happy and others sad depending on the mood. Created by the Jewish religious community, it is adapted as a basis for songs in the Jewish Theater where words are added as part of the tune. I like the way these songs have a soulful sound to them. Sitting back and listening to the voices, you can't help but be touched by the emotion.

Menus to Get You Started

When it comes to preparing a meal for family and friends for any occasion, the hardest decisions have to do with planning a menu. Finding the perfect balance comes with practice, and to make it easier for you, I've listed a few of my suggestions. Soon you will come up with your own planning ideas for menus of which you will be proud.

Traditional Shabbos Dinner for Friday Evening

Wine or grape juice (for the Kiddush blessing)
Challah
Gefilte Fish (page 94) with Homemade Horse-
    radish (page 57)
Chicken Soup with Matzo Balls (page 60)
Roast Chicken (page 102)
Potato Kugel (page 164)
Green vegetable
Stewed Bartlett Pears with Apples and Cinnamon
    (page 202)

Shabbos Lunch for Saturday Afternoon

Wine or grape juice (for the Kiddush blessing)
Challah
Cholent (page 127)
Cucumber and Scallion Salad with Fresh Dill
    (page 56)
Sugar Kichlach (page 193)

Rosh Hashana (Jewish New Year's)

Round Challah
Apples and honey
Chopped Chicken Liver (page 36)
Chicken Soup (page 60) with noodles
Bubbe's Brisket (page 114)
Beef or Vegetarian Tzimis (page 120 or 121)
Green vegetable
Honey Cake (page 173)
Pomegranate

The Meal Before the Yom Kippur Fast

Round Challah
Gefilte Fish (page 94)
Chicken with kreplach or noodles
Roast Chicken (page 102) or Tasty Soup Chicken
    (page 108)
Rice
Vegetable
Tea
Honey Cake (page 173)

The Meal After the Yom Kippur Fast

(Part 1)

Tshaynik milk (see box on page 42) or tea
Challah with butter or margarine
Pickled herring or Chopped Herring (page 41)

(Part 2)

Plain Chicken Soup (page 60) or Chicken Soup
    with noodles
Leftovers from the meal before the fast
Pineapple Sponge Cake (page 174)

Meal for Succos

Gefilte Fish (page 94) or Mock Chopped
    Chicken Liver (page 38)
Mushroom Barley Bean Soup (page 79)
Stuffed Cabbage (page 124)
Mashed potatoes
Marble Mandel Bread (page 168)

Chanukah Menu for the Festival of Lights

Potato Latkes (page 155) with sour cream
  and applesauce
Easy Baked Fish (page 88)
Bubbe's Noodle Kugel (page 152)

Purim Menu

Chopped Eggs and Onions (page 39)
Sweet and Sour Turkey Drumsticks (page 112)
Chicken Soup (page 60) with kreplach
Jelly Jammies (page 182)

Shalach Manos (Small Gift Baskets Given to Friends and Neighbors on Purim)

Small bottle of grape juice or wine
Hamantaschen (page 200)
Orange or apple

Passover Seder Plate

Charoset for Passover (page 46)
Homemade Horseradish (page 57)
Parsley or romaine lettuce
Roasted shankbone
Hard-boiled egg
Bowl of salt water

Passover Meal

Wine or grape juice
Matzo
Gefilte Fish (page 94)
Chicken Soup (with optional Matzo Balls
  [page 60] or matzo farfel)
Bubbe's Brisket (page 114)
Vegetarian Tzimis (page 121)
Potato Kugel (page 164)
Chocolate-Orange Wine Cake (page 190) or
  Lime-Laced Fruit Salad (page 54)

Passover Breakfast

Stuffed Matzo Meal Latkes (Pancakes) (page 19)
Savory Matzo Brei (Fried Matzo) (page 18)

Shavuot Meal (Festival of Receiving the Torah)

Eggplant Lasagna (page 158) or Baked Fish
  Cakes (page 90)

Blueberry Coffee Cake (Blueberry Buckle)
  (page 26)
Cheese, Apple, or Blueberry Blintzes (page 20)
Bubbe's Noodle Kugel (page 152)
Serve with your favorite vegetables and other
  dairy items

Hors d'Ouevres Party

Salmon Puff Pastry Bites (page 40)
Mini Blintzes (page 50)
Mock Chopped Chicken Liver (page 38)
Holiday Cookies (page 176)
Jelly Jammies (page 182)
Sugar Kichlach (page 193)

Picnic Lunch

Half-Sour Pickles (page 52)
Bubbe's Burgers (page 82) or Crispy Baked
  Chicken (page 105)
Four-Bean Salad (page 157)
Lemonade

Bubbe's Get-Well-Soon Remedies

Chicken Soup with Matzo Balls (page 60)
Tomato, Lettuce, and Onion Sandwich (page 84)
Gogul Mogul (page 63)

Dinner for Beginners (Meat)

Chicken Rice Casserole (page 106)
Vegetable
Salad
Apple Cake (page 197)

Dinner for Beginners (Dairy)

Cream of Broccoli Soup (page 70)
Baked Honey Mustard Salmon (page 89)
Baked potato
Salad
Bubbe's Noodle Kugel (page 152)

Meal for Vegetarians

Vegetarian Stew (page 74)
Salad
Eggless Chocolate Cake (page 189)

Cooking Words for Beginners

To help the beginners who are not familiar with common cooking terms, here is a list of a few important cooking words you should know to get you started. I hope this will inspire you to take a closer look, expand your cooking vocabulary, and try out recipes. All you need is a little understanding and practice.

Bake: Cooking with dry heat in an oven. Used, for example, with cakes and pastries.

Baste: Take the sauce or liquid with a spoon or brush from the cooking pot and pour over the meat so it won't dry out.

Beat: To use a hand beater or food mixer and mix with a fast motion, mixing ingredients together.

Blend: Combining ingredients together gently.

Boil: Place a pot with liquid, which is generally water, on a burner on high until it reaches a point in which there are bubbles jumping up and down. This is known as the boiling point. Generally used for soups.

Braise: To brown the meat a little in a Dutch oven or heavy pot on all sides and use very little water in cooking. It is generally used for pot roast or any meat that is tough and needs a long time to cook, such as beef stews.

Broil: Generally the top rack in the oven used to cook the meat directly under high heat in a very short period of time, such as steaks and fish.

Chop: To cut into small pieces.

Coat: To cover the food with flour or egg or with breadcrumbs or matzo meal, such as schnitzel.

Core: To remove seeds from the center of fruit or vegetables.

Cream: Generally blending sugar and margarine or butter together used mostly for cakes.

Dice: Cut into small cube pieces and have them all look about the same size.

Drain: Pour the liquid out of whatever you are currently cooking, such as boiled potatoes for mashing or vegetables after cooking.

Egg wash: A combination of water and egg used for coating meats and vegetables or the surface of baked goods before baking or coating with breadcrumbs.

Fold: Especially used in baking, generally means to combine the beaten egg whites and the rest of a cake mixture. It is done in a very slow motion with a spoon or other kitchen tool bringing the mixture from the bottom over the top of the other mixture so that no air is lost in blending both together. For example, Pineapple Sponge Cake (page 174).

Fry: Cooking food in a vegetable oil or butter or margarine, generally done in a frying pan.

Grate: To grind food into fine pieces by rubbing it over a grater. Typically used with bread, vegetables, and fruit, especially the skin of oranges and lemons.

Grease: To coat a frying pan lightly with butter, margarine, or vegetable oil as you would in making blintzes or latkes.

Knead: To work and continuously fold over the dough until it is smooth and ready.

Marinade: A mixture of vinegar, water, oil, seasonings, and spices mixed together with meat placed in the mixture for a certain length of time so that the meat develops a special flavor.

Mash: Using a fork or spoon to crush food so that it is soft and without lumps. Example would be potatoes used in the Baked Fish Cakes recipe (page 90).

Melt: Placing a solid food in the microwave or other heat source so that the heat will dissolve it into a liquid.

Mince: To cut up into extremely fine pieces.

Preheat: To heat a frying pan before placing ingredients in it. Also used with an oven to get the temperature to the exact degree needed before placing food into the oven.

Roast: To cook meat or chicken in the oven without a cover.

Sauté: Frying food in a small amount of vegetable oil in a frying pan stirring continuously so that it does not burn and yet helps develop a good taste.

Sear: To brown the outside of the meat quickly at high temperature at the beginning of cooking so that it will seal in the juices before starting the rest of the cooking procedure.

Season: Adding salt, pepper, and spices to improve the flavor.

Shred: To pull apart or cut into thin pieces with a knife or a grater.

Sift: To mix dry ingredients together through a sifter, such as ingredients for a cake.

Simmer: After a food has started to cook bring it down to the lowest cooking level so that it will just barely boil with continuous heat, such as a soup that you have to cook for several hours.

Skim: To remove foam or fat from the top of cooking soup or stew.

Stew: To cook slowly with liquid until the food is tender, for example lamb stew in cholent, tzimis, etc.

Stir: Mixing the ingredients together slowly so that they will all blend.

Stuff: To fill the opening with a combination of breadcrumbs and other ingredients. An example is Stuffed Breast of Veal (page 136).

Toss: To mix ingredients together gently, such as with a salad.

Truss: To close an opening that has been stuffed using a trussing needle or skewers.

Zest: The outer skin of a lemon or orange finely grated with a grater or zester.

Formulas for Metric Conversion

FORMULAS FOR METRIC CONVERSION

Ounces to grams	multiply ounces by 28.35
Pounds to grams	multiply pounds by 453.5
Cups to liters	multiply cups by .24
Fahrenheit to Centigrade	subtract 32 from Fahrenheit, multiply by 5 and divide by 9

METRIC EQUIVALENTS FOR VOLUME

U.S.	Metric		U.S.	Metric	
$\frac{1}{8}$ tsp.	0.6 ml	—	$\frac{1}{3}$ cup	79 ml	—
$\frac{1}{4}$ tsp.	1.2 ml	—	$\frac{1}{2}$ cup	118 ml	4 fl. oz
$\frac{1}{2}$ tsp.	2.5 ml	—	$\frac{2}{3}$ cup	158 ml	—
$\frac{3}{4}$ tsp.	3.7 ml	—	$\frac{3}{4}$ cup	178 ml	6 fl. oz
1 tsp.	5 ml	—	1 cup	237 ml	8 fl. oz
$1\frac{1}{2}$ tsp.	7.4 ml	—	$1\frac{1}{4}$ cups	300 ml	—
2 tsp.	10 ml	—	$1\frac{1}{2}$ cups	355 ml	—
1 Tbsp.	15 ml	—	$1\frac{3}{4}$ cups	425 ml	—
$1\frac{1}{2}$ Tbsp.	22 ml	—	2 cups (1 pint)	500 ml	16 fl. oz
2 Tbsp. ($\frac{1}{8}$ cup)	30 ml	1 fl. oz	3 cups	725 ml	—
3 Tbsp.	45 ml	—	4 cups (1 quart)	.95 liters	32 fl. oz
$\frac{1}{4}$ cup	59 ml	2 fl. oz	16 cups (1 gallon)	3.8 liters	128 fl. oz

METRIC EQUIVALENTS FOR BUTTER

U.S.	Metric
2 tsp.	9.4 g
1 Tbsp.	14 g
1½ Tbsp.	21 g
2 Tbsp. (1 oz)	28 g
3 Tbsp.	42 g
4 Tbsp.	57 g
4 oz. (1 stick)	113 g
8 oz. (2 sticks)	226 g

METRIC EQUIVALENTS FOR LENGTH

U.S.	Metric
¼ inch	.65 cm
½ inch	1.25 cm
1 inch	2.50 cm
2 inches	5.00 cm
3 inches	6.00 cm
4 inches	8.00 cm
5 inches	11.00 cm
6 inches	15.00 cm
7 inches	18.00 cm
8 inches	20.00 cm
9 inches	23.00 cm
12 inches	30.50 cm
15 inches	38.00 cm

OVEN TEMPERATURES

Degrees Fahrenheit	Degrees Centigrade	British Gas Marks
200°	93°	—
250°	120°	½
275°	140°	1
300°	150°	2
325°	165°	3
350°	175°	4
375°	190°	5
400°	200°	6
450°	230°	8

METRIC EQUIVALENTS FOR WEIGHT

U.S.	Metric
1 oz	28 g
2 oz	57 g
3 oz	85 g
4 oz (¼ lb)	113 g
5 oz	142 g
6 oz	170 g
7 oz	198 g
8 oz (½ lb)	227 g
12 oz (¾ lb)	340 g
14 oz	397 g
16 oz (1 lb)	454 g
2.2 lbs	1 kg

Source: Herbst, Sharon Tyler. *The Food Lover's Companion.* 3rd ed. Hauppauge: Barron's, 2001.

Epilogue

We have almost reached the end of the book! I hope that you enjoyed making the food and reading the stories that have accumulated from my childhood up until today. I didn't realize how important looking back at all of these memories was, and I have stacks of papers and photos all over the house to show for it.

In fact one incident happened recently that really made me realize why everyone feels such a strong connection to *Feed Me Bubbe*. I had a home-theater consultant from a popular store over the house, because Zadie's been thinking about getting a new television set. Seeing the consultant's reaction as he walked through my home really put everything in perspective. Even his expression as he took a look at my current television set and remarked how it must be from around the 1980s really made me realize how lucky I am to still be able to use the technology of my day today. As Avrom and the consultant were speaking back and forth in a technology language I couldn't really understand, I was proud of the conversation that they were having together. It really is amazing how far everything has come along since we first got our home.

With all the new technology today, there is a sense of loss in the traditions and values that I grew up with. This is why I have honored the fans' wishes and not disclosed where I live, careful of what information that I provide, and even just go by the name of Bubbe and nothing more. When I see an email or Facebook message or YouTube response come in asking if they can be adopted by me I can now understand why.

I want to give you, all of my adopted ones, a very special gift. I have a cookbook from a long time ago. At the end of the book, the author mentions to "fill in your own special family recipes here" on it in big capital letters. I took advantage of this, and as I perfected special recipes on my own, I wrote them in the book. I even saved newspaper clippings which I used to help make my own style of cooking. I want to give you that same opportunity that I had. When you make something in the kitchen that you really love, please write it down on the blank notebook pages in the back. When you look back you can truly say that Bubbe has adopted you as you carry this book with you through your own journey.

On behalf of Avrom and myself, thank you for an incredible journey.

Es Gezunterhait (to your good health),
Bubbe
646-402-5231
http://www.feedmebubbe.com
http://www.facebook.com/FeedMeBubbe
feedme@chalutzproductions.com
AOL Instant Messenger: feedmebubbe

Index

Notes

Notes

Notes

Notes

Notes

Notes